This is where you would normally find opinions and quotes from a bunch of people who say they read the book and liked it. But really, the only opinion that matters is yours.

So read the book and see what you think.

HOW ORDINARY PEOPLE CAN ACHIEVE OUTRAGEOUS SUCCESS

EDGY

CONVERSATIONS

GET BEYOND THE NONSENSE IN YOUR LIFE AND DO WHAT REALLY MATTERS

DAN WALDSCHMIDT

EDGY CONVERSATIONS
How Ordinary People Can Achieve Outrageous Success

Next Century Publishing
www.NextCenturyPublishing.com

Printed in the United States of America
ISBN-10: 0989533107
ISBN-13: 978-0-9895331-0-2

Credits
Developmental and Contributing Editor: Juli Baldwin,
  The Baldwin Group, Juli@BaldwinGrp.com
Book Design: Cecilia Sorochin, SoroDesign.
Book Production: Melissa Cabana, Back Porch Creative,
  melissa@backporchcreative.com
Cover and Illustrations: Justin Gammon

CONTENTS

PROLOGUE
HOW IT ALL STARTED

I
can still
remember the
oily taste of
cool metal on
my tongue.

I was 25 years old and wanted to die. I just wanted the pain to go away.

I sat on the steps of my garage that day, a gun in my mouth, wallowing in a drunken haze of bitter, self-destructive hopelessness.

I'd had it all. But I'd screwed up everything.

All I'd ever wanted was to be amazing... outrageous... extraordinary.

I'd wanted to make a difference in the world.

And there was no denying that I'd already accomplished a lot.

By the time I was 22, I was known as "Boy Wonder" around Washington, D.C. circles – the CEO of a fast-growing company that was expanding up and down the East Coast and doing work all over the world.

I was married to a magnificent woman, had a beautiful son and lived in a house way too big for the three of us.

And to those who didn't dig any deeper behind the facade of thousand-dollar suits and smooth answers, I seemed to have it all together.

But inside I was a mess of self-doubt and guilt. And I was tired.

Despite my obsessive compulsion for extreme sports and my tendency to work maniacal hours – often not coming home for days – I had lost my ability to bend the world to my will.

My marriage was in a million pieces. Broken. Busted. As horribly screwed up as you can imagine. And I felt all the jagged edges of the disaster.

I hadn't been around for my wife, and so someone else had stepped in. For a while I was able to pretend that it wasn't happening, that it didn't matter to me.

But there is something cruelly crippling about knowing someone else has taken your place.

And that drove me mad.

I blamed her. I cursed her. I tried to throw her out.

So what if I didn't have time to spend with her?

But a part of me knew that my selfish behavior – my inability to show love – had screwed up an amazing relationship.

I couldn't pretend anymore that this whole twisted drama wasn't tearing my heart out piece by piece.

It wasn't like I'd never screwed up anything before.

I had failed a zillion times before this. But I had always thought of failure as simply "not yet successful." I had always assumed success was inevitable. And it kinda was.

But this time it was personal. This one felt final.

And it was maddening, because I couldn't change the situation by myself. I had always been able to solve any issue or problem or challenge by outworking everyone else with raw, superhuman, highly focused passion.

This was out of my control. I couldn't make her be faithful to me. Or love me.

And the pain was **unimaginable.**

That's probably not how it looked from the outside though.

See, I didn't want to lose her...but not really for the right reasons. I never wanted to lose anything. For any reason. Ever.

And so I changed my ways for a few months...just long enough to show that I was the honorable person in the family. I went through the motions. I spent more time with her. I took her out to expensive restaurants and on fancy shopping trips.

And I expected my three months of Boy Scout behavior to earn me instantaneous love and respect. I even told her as much.

That drove her even further away.

So I reverted to the only thing I'd ever been really good at: extreme behavior.

I worked longer. I swore louder. I trained harder.

I spent every waking moment trying to escape from the pain.

Day after day, I shut the door to my office and cried at my desk. My assistant would gently knock on the door and remind me that I had meetings. I would clean myself up, adjust my tie and go put together amazing business deals.

But inside I was becoming unhinged. I was an emotional wreck. That just meant I needed to push myself even harder.

So I did.

I pushed myself to exhaustion and beyond. At one point, I lost 20 pounds in just a few days.

Through all the relentless training at the gym, I caught a staph infection. But initially no one was able to diagnose it.

For four days, I lay in the emergency room at the hospital. They brought in infectious disease specialists and checked my blood for AIDS and other auto-immune diseases. I was all clear. They couldn't figure out what was wrong.

Their only option was to try different antibiotics. When one didn't work, they tried another. And another. And then another. Eventually I began to recover.

But my body was broken. I was weak and out of shape. Everything I had worked for was gone.

And that just added to my torment.

I'd always been able to count on myself to perform. No matter how insurmountable the challenge, I'd always pushed myself hard enough to overcome it. But for the first time in my life, I wasn't physically able to perform.

It was bad enough that I had let my family down. Now I'd let myself down. The only friend I had left (myself) had deserted me. And it was hauntingly lonely.

My sense of failure completely engulfed me. The wild thoughts in my head became all-consuming.

This time I was beaten. It was time to end the game.

The staph infection had almost killed me. Now I wanted to do it myself.

And that is how I came to be standing in the middle of my garage, outrageously drunk, with a glass of whiskey in one hand and a gun in the other.

As the tears began to run down my face, my sadness turned into sobs. It was a sweeping sadness so deeply painful that I knew I wanted to die. There was no other escape. I wanted out.

Blinking away the tears, I grabbed a box of bullets.

In a twisted, overachiever kind of way – after all, one alone would do the job – I shoved bullet after bullet into the clip of my Browning .22 pistol until it was full.

I took another slug of whiskey and staggered to the back steps of the garage. Sitting down, I set the glass a little too forcefully on the step beside me, but it didn't break.

For just a few seconds, that observation took my mind off my overwhelming sadness.

But soon it all came rushing back.

I picked up the pistol and raised it to my head. Curiously, I questioned whether I should place it at my temple or in my mouth. Would I screw this up as well?

I decided my mouth was a sure bet.

I knew I was serious when the taste of gun oil hit my senses. Part of me wondered if I would actually do it. The other part just wanted it all to be over. I was tired of hurting.

Soon the pain would be gone. I nodded, as if confirming to myself that this was the right thing to do.

I
placed my
finger on the
trigger and
began to
pull...

YOU DON'T NEED
ANOTHER BOOK ON SUCCESS

You don't need another book on success. You don't.

You already know almost everything you need to know about achieving success: Set goals. Work hard. Be persistent. And don't give up until you get what you want. It's all stuff you could probably repeat in your sleep.

And it's something I know a little bit about.

I know how to do all that success stuff. I'm a 2-time college dropout. I should never have made a penny. Yet I've made millions and millions of dollars. (And lost a lot, too.)

As an executive, I drove massive sales growth for a decade. As a consultant, I've taught businesses all over the world to do the same.

I became a CEO at age 25. But I'm not an entrepreneur. I got into the business and worked my way up.

I know how to break the rules and be a superstar – not just in business, but in life.

But I'm not special.

I'm just an ordinary dude who did some pretty extraordinary things.

And achieved some outrageous success.

But this isn't a book about your typical success-advice nonsense. It's about the baggage between your ears that keeps making you fail.

And that's something I know a lot about.

There are hundreds, if not thousands, of books on success

and high performance. What is missing is the real-world, gut-wrenching discussion about the emotional challenges of success – a focus on attitudes instead of just actions.

And that is a huge void. Because your actions will fail until you master the deeply personal aspects of your life that drive those actions.

The hard truth is that success isn't a series of actions. It is an attitude.

Success is not about what you do. It's about who you are.

Everything you want to achieve for yourself – all those goals and dreams and wishes – will come as a result of who you are, not what you do.

So rather than teaching you how to "do" success, we're going to talk about how to "be."

This is not yet another book telling you to do this and do that and you'll make a zillion dollars. That's not what this is all about. (Although that might exactly be your result.)

This book is about the uncomfortably powerful truths you won't find in your typical "success" book. It's a look behind the scenes at pain, fear, love – yes, love – and the other key attitudes that drive huge success, regardless of the success "process" that you use.

It's about who you are, why you're not where you want to be, and how to live a life of outrageous opportunity.

It's a return to what really works.

It's about how you – an ordinary person like me – can be extraordinary, whether you are leading a company, selling deals or training for the Olympics.

What you read here will change the rest of your life. You'll exceed every expectation you have for yourself. You'll set even more outrageous goals. You'll be happier.

And you'll have a deeper sense of satisfaction for it all. You won't be able to help it.

I purposely kept this book as brief as possible. It's short

because the true essentials of high performance are pretty concise. In fact, this entire book could be a single word:

But that might be a little too short.

The idea of "being" a better version of you is a pretty inspiring concept. There is something ultimately satisfying about being all you can be.

And only you know the full potential of what that could be.

But I can tell you this: It's bigger than you have ever imagined.

That brings up a question you need to ask yourself: Who and what do you want to be...and why?

Take a moment and let that sink in. It's a bigger question than it seems.

Unfortunately, I learned the answer the hard way.

And there's something else I learned.

You can't fake it.

You have to feel it. You have to live it. You have to be consumed by it. That's what makes you successful.

And what is *"it"*? What is this attitude that you need to have?

It's obsession. That determination – that grit – is the deciding factor in your eventual success.

See, you can't avoid future obstacles. They are inevitable.

You're going to get beat up. You're going to take an uppercut to the chin and hit the floor.

And it will likely happen when you least expect it. When your hands aren't up and your feet aren't set.

And that's why what you've done in the past – and what you will do in the future – don't matter!

In that moment when you are lying bloodied on the canvas, it's who you are that matters. It's what is inside you that makes the difference.

It's raw courage that gets you up off the floor.

There's no magic success formula for that. No super-special "7-step" action plan.

Just an insane obsession to get back up.

And the more you will yourself to get back up and the better you clean yourself up, the faster you will find yourself stumbling toward the finish line you call success.

It takes heart.

Not brains. Not brawn.

Guts.

Because success isn't about knowing more. It's about being more.

And that's not a list you can download off the Internet or a blog post you can re-tweet or a business strategy you can duplicate from a best-selling business book.

You have to be more. You have to desperately want more. You have to care more.

The reality is that you already know what to do. That's never been a serious question anyway.

The real question is, *what will you do about it?*

Who will you choose to become?

Let's talk about it.

STOP MAKING EXCUSES
FOR WHO – AND WHERE – YOU ARE

What you do matters.

Everything. The big stuff. The little stuff. Even the annoying stuff.

It matters that you waste time. It matters that you blame others for your failures. It matters that you are lazy at times.

It matters because achieving your goals matters. And eliminating excuses is the pathway that takes you there. It's the same path that every great achiever has followed.

Sigmund Freud was booed off the stage the first time he presented his theories to a group of scientists in Europe. He went on to win the Goethe Award for his work in psychology.

Winston Churchill, one of the greatest leaders of the twentieth century, wasn't even elected by the people when he became Prime Minister at the age of 65. He was appointed by the King when the previous Prime Minister received a vote of "no confidence."

Albert Einstein didn't speak until he was four, couldn't read basic words until he was seven and was expelled from school. He eventually revolutionized physics with his Theory of Relativity.

Henry Ford failed at farming, at being an apprentice and as a machinist and went bankrupt five times. Yet he modernized mass production.

Stan Smith was rejected as a ball boy for a Davis Cup tennis match because he was "too clumsy." He won eight Davis Cup championships and is considered one of the greatest doubles tennis players of all time.

Charles Schultz had every cartoon rejected that he submitted to his high school yearbook. He was rejected by Walt Disney. He went on to create the most popular cartoon series ever: Peanuts.

Vincent Van Gogh only sold a single painting his entire life – to a friend's sister for about $50. He painted over 800 masterpieces, seven of which are together worth almost $1 billion.

Leo Tolstoy flunked out of law school and was labeled "unable to learn" by his professors. He went on to become one of the world's greatest novelists (think *War and Peace*).

John Creasey failed as a salesman, a desk clerk, a factory worker and an aspiring writer, getting 754 rejection notices from publishers. He wrote more than 600 novels and is considered one of the greatest mystery writers ever.

Hank Aaron failed his tryout with the Brooklyn Dodgers and went 0-5 in his first game in the majors. He went on to set the Major League Baseball record for homeruns and held that record for 33 years.

Living excuse-free is about taking responsibility for every aspect of your life. It's about creating a future you're proud of.

So what if it hasn't been done before?
Be the first.

So what if you get it wrong a few times?
Reinvent yourself.

So what if you don't have a college degree?
Be curious. Learn more.

So what if no one believes in you?
You don't need approval to be successful.

So what if it gets hard?
All big things require pain and loss.

So what if you keep trying and never get it right?
Audacity is always the right move.

So what if people aren't following you?
They will follow once you do something amazing.

So what if you get hurt?
That's the price of boldness.

So what if you're under-appreciated?
Ego would only make you complacent.

So what if everything you thought was right turns out to be wrong?
Make up new rules.

So what if the experts disagree with you?
The experts might be wrong.

So what if you give more than you get?
You might just be happier.

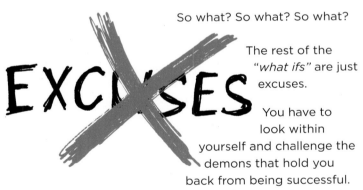

So what? So what? So what?

The rest of the *"what ifs"* are just excuses.

You have to look within yourself and challenge the demons that hold you back from being successful. You'll never rise to be a champion until you can look past the fear and the failure and the excuses holding you back.

That starts with you believing that you can be amazing regardless of who or where you are in life right now.

Carl "Sugarfoot" Joseph was born in Madison, FL, a little east of the state capital. The fourth of ten children, he was raised by a single mom. They were a poor family living in the country without any real access to recreation or sports facilities.

And that's probably why Carl worked so hard to become a star athlete. Growing up, he played basketball and street football. He fought with the older boys, and it taught him to be tough. He would get thrown violently to the ground but spring back up and launch himself back into the action.

In seventh grade, he made the basketball team. Standing under the rim, he would jump straight up and dunk the basketball. And that was just the beginning.

In high school, he played basketball and football and ran track, setting records in almost every sport. At one track event, he high jumped 5'8" then turned around and threw the shotput 40 feet and the discus 130 feet. And in one football game against much bigger, double-teaming opponents, Carl exploded with 11 tackles, an interception and a blocked punt.

The young superstar didn't let down one bit as he made the transition to college. He played middle linebacker at Bethune-Cookman University, where five of his teammates went on to play in the NFL. The Wildcats won their conference championship, and a lot of it had to do with the inspiration that came directly from Carl.

You see, Carl was born without a left leg.

Every competition Carl participated in was a lopsided event: everyone else running, turning and jumping on two feet while Carl did it all hopping on one. No prosthesis. No crutch.

Just heart.

When asked by an interviewer what his limitations were, Carl said, "I don't have any."

So...**what was your excuse again?**

Eliminating excuses is important because your future is important.

If you only get the future that you work for, then what you work on is pretty important, right?

You probably don't want to screw that up.

If there is a list of things to not flub, "your future" has to be high on the list.

Your decisions lead to your destiny.

Do you believe that? You should. It's true.

Sooner or later, what you do – and who you really are – determines what you ultimately achieve.

What does that really mean?

Let's get practical about it. Let's talk about how much sleep you really need and how a decision like that impacts your results.

Getting up earlier means you have more time to conquer the world. Simply getting up 1 hour earlier every day for 50 years equates to an extra 2,281 business days – or 6.25 years – of conquest.

You win more when you fight more.

Your daily decisions – or the excuses you make – add up over time.

It's easy to say that working hard is important. We all know that, right? But just because you say the words doesn't mean you're doing the "doing" part.

Your future is about the decisions you make – not the ideas you have.

It's causal rather than casual. You actually have a say in what you achieve.

We all want that extra 6.25 years of conquest. But when we have a zillion minute-by-minute considerations just to decide whether to stay in bed or to get up and "conquer," most of us choose comfort. It seems small at the time – after all, it's just one hour. But the results are life changing. Literally.

The decisions that you make hundreds of times a day build

your future. They all count.

So, how can you change your future, today?

Start by believing that you matter. That what you do matters. That what you do right now changes the possibilities for your future.

It's a mindset. (An "edgy" mindset, in case you were wondering.)

It means that you:

Choose to be positive when things are scary;

Fight to win even when you just got the wind knocked out of you;

Are honest even if it means you'll be embarrassed;

Take the time to learn new skills, new talents and new ideas when it's easier to just "be you;"

Invest in personal inspiration instead of letting anxiety drive your decisions.

The importance of eliminating excuses is in understanding the outcome of individual decisions.

Being positive 20 times a day for 15 years is 109,500 opportunities to create a happier future.

Winning 1 more time per year could mean 30 amazing, mind-blowing successes over a lifetime.

Telling the truth just 1 more time each day gives you 365 more reasons a year to trust yourself.

Reading 1 new book per week for 22 years equates to 1,144 new ideas from the smartest minds in the world.

Creating 5 new meaningful (non-Facebook/Twitter) relationships per month over 35 years is 2,100 new people you can count on when you really need help.

A lot of small choices make a big difference.

What if you had 109,500 happier moments, 30 more successes, 365 more ways to trust yourself, 1,144 new ideas and 2,100 new friends?

Could you conquer more? Could you do some outrageous things?

Possibly.

Probably.

You can bet on it.

So stop making excuses.

EDGY CONVERSATIONS

So there I was...sitting on the back steps of my garage...tears running down the sides of my face...the barrel of a gun in my mouth and my finger on the trigger.

So much pain in my heart. I just wanted the pain to go away.

I had a flash of clarity:

If I pull the trigger, there's no going back. It's over...for real.

There would be no romantic ending to this decision. No Hollywood plotline. This was real life. And it was gritty and nasty.

My "Why am I doing this?" shouted at me, and I had no good answer.

I pulled the gun out of my mouth and thought about it...did I really want to die?

Maybe I didn't.

More than anything, I wanted to be whole again. I wanted to put the pieces back together.

Maybe it was the whiskey talking, but I wanted to figure out the meaning of life and love and success and happiness. Because everything I had always thought was important, wasn't.

Through the pain and the tears and my own insanity, I saw myself for who I was.

And as much as I didn't want to admit it, I knew deep down that I was horribly at fault. My own bad habits had caused this mess, and my passive aggression in the middle of the drama only made the mess worse.

And that realization was deeply saddening.

21

I had the clear sense that I could give in and stop trying, or I could stop being selfish and try to figure this whole thing out.

Sure, I was drunk. And hardly in the right frame of mind to be making life-changing breakthroughs. But things started to come together in my mind. As emotionally illogical as I was, I knew that I wanted to change. I needed to change.

But I didn't have the answers. In fact, I wasn't even sure I knew where to get the answers. And I knew there was no easy way to solve the problems I had created for myself.

I just knew that this was going to be the biggest struggle of my life.

The rest of that night was a blur. I fell asleep. Or passed out. I wasn't conscious – that much I know.

And frankly, I don't remember what happened after that. I don't. I can't tell you what happened the next day or the next week.

It was a confusing splash of trying to fix my relationship with my wife and keep it all together. All the while searching for answers, looking for hope.

And the more I looked, the more I found.

I began to notice that I wasn't the only person in pain. In fact, the more I looked, the more I began to see the fear and pain and loss all around me.

Broken people. Hurting people. Successful people. All looking for how to solve the problems of life and love and greatness.

People you would meet at a dinner party and admire. People you would think had it all together.

But they didn't. And neither did I.

I thought a lot about how the fear and pain I was feeling was the same fear and pain I saw in others. And I thought about my life...and who I thought I was.

From the time I was 4 or 5, my parents began to drill into me the concept of mastery – the idea that anything can be conquered. You just have to be willing to go further than anyone else.

That was the seed of my extreme behavior and extreme discipline.

I started my first business – mowing lawns – when I was 12. I had thousands of self-earned dollars in the bank by the time I graduated from high school.

I went to college...twice.

I dropped out...twice.

I first went to seminary but left after three years. I later quit college after studying government and international politics for two years. I got good grades but I was bored. What I was studying didn't seem to matter. I memorized everything I needed to know and spit it back out at test time.

My first job in college was selling cemetery plots to aging adults. Talk about edgy! Soon after that I got my insurance license so I could offer health and life insurance packages. Both were completely new and utterly fascinating sales ventures.

I hustled. I failed a lot.

For every success I've had over the years, I've had an equal number of disasters. Plus a ten- to twenty-fold return of plain-vanilla failures.

But I also had some huge wins. Some unbelievable wins, in fact.

That sense of "never say die" and "nothing is impossible" stayed with me. I learned that if I never stopped trying – if I kept trying new things and ideas – I was unstoppable.

That early foundation – understanding the relationship between effort and curiosity and success – set the groundwork for what would evolve into my role as a young CEO and a decade of massive sales growth.

In my early 20s, I transformed a few businesses. I helped a plumbing company grow their sales 900% in just a few years. (Imagine trying to make manual labor look sexy!)

It was fun to be a part of.

Then I joined a tiny company that provided services to law firms. We grew it by millions of dollars the first year alone – 7,900% sales growth, actually. Ludicrous, isn't it? But that's what we did.

They couldn't pay me a decent salary, so I negotiated a percentage of sales. Good call.

The owners made me CEO. I was 25, full of ideas and determined to change an entire industry. We did that, too.

On the side, I was doing some pretty wild international deals. And in my spare time I trained for cage fighting.

People always said I couldn't accomplish all of what I did. They said I was crazy to think I could. That was me – the crazy guy with the out-of-the-box thinking, making big things happen.

I put in massive amounts of effort. That was my trump card.

I figured there were plenty of people that could out-smart me, but I knew that I could out-last and out-suffer anyone when it came to putting in hard work. I broke my competitors with sheer human effort.

I knew how to do extreme behavior. But it was all focused in the wrong direction. I didn't know how to channel it. Sure, I was successful. But I was a jerk. And I caused a lot of collateral damage along the way.

For years I'd done every crazy thing possible to prove that I was unstoppable. But ultimately, I'd been stopped by my own behavior and misguided intentions.

Now, I tell you all of this not to say, "Look at how great I am," but to explain that I thought I knew a lot about how to achieve success. But it wasn't the kind of success that really meant anything.

I figured out in dramatic fashion that success and happiness aren't tied to the size of your house or your bank account.

There is nothing wrong with having wealth. But money doesn't maintain relationships. Achievements don't mend wounds.

In my quest to heal myself, I desperately wanted to understand how others had achieved true success. So I studied people who had accomplished outrageous feats of greatness against overwhelming obstacles.

And I discovered something pretty fascinating.

Most successful people are just ordinary people who do extraordinary things.

That is what makes them successful.

Think about it.

Throughout all of time, it's been ordinary people who achieved outrageous success.

Sure there is the occasional child prodigy or someone born with enormous mental capacity or raw physical talent.

But nearly all of those whom we would universally call successful were not born with amazing natural talent or a silver spoon in their mouth. They were ordinary people who pulled themselves together and became awesome.

They weren't born with greatness. They became great.

In my search for answers, I learned some other interesting things.

Namely, that success is an attitude.

Success is about who you are,
not what you do or what you have.

And I observed that successful people all share the same four attributes.

They aren't afraid to be **Extreme**.

They are **Disciplined**.

They are **Giving**.

And they understand the **Y(h)uman factor.**

In my lingo, they are EDGY.

All of the successful people I observed had these four qualities. Education wasn't a key differentiator. Neither was upbringing, religion, race or family wealth.

The first two I had down pat. It was through extreme behavior and unrelenting discipline that I had achieved all my early material success. (I even have "Live Extreme" tattooed on my arm.)

But without the Giving mindset and the Y(h)uman element, I had destroyed myself, my marriage and a whole lot of other things along the way.

I wasn't good at the Giving part. If I gave favors, it was because I wanted to be able to "call them in" down the road. It was tit for tat – strategic trading – not giving from the heart.

Sure, I understood the Y(h)uman factor. I knew what made people tick and how to get them to perform at their peak. But I used it to manipulate rather than motivate.

Today I know that extreme behavior, if not contained, is like a nuclear bomb. You may accomplish your goal, but at what cost?

You have to have all four characteristics to achieve outrageous, healthy success.

Not only do you have to work harder and longer than you ever expected, you also have to give more and love more than you ever anticipated.

Look, the ugly truth is that no one really knows for sure what works when it comes to achieving greatness. Even the "experts" can't agree.

We all struggle with this idea of how to be successful, whether CEO, mom or college student.

We're all looking for the answers. I bet you are, too.

You read the books. You go to the conferences and listen to the experts.

You follow the seven-step program.

You scan the top blogs by the leading gurus.

You check out webinars to get the latest tips and tricks.

You join a networking group to see what other people are doing.

You hire a coach to help you achieve your goals.

You start a "high achiever" group on LinkedIn.

You work your butt off.

And at the end of the day, you feel like you are no closer to success.

Something is missing.

Maybe you are missing what I was missing.

Maybe you need to be more EDGY.

EDGY is how ordinary people can become extraordinary.

EDGY is how you can achieve outrageous success.

Are you ready to be **EDGY**?

EXTREME
BEHAVIOR

Here's a harsh reality: **We're just not tough enough.**

It was World War II. A team of soldiers in the American Infantry Division was fighting inch by inch for a painfully embattled strip of tropical island in the South Pacific. Day after day they fought, losing men and gaining little headway. As the days dragged on, their supplies ran lower, and several of the men started getting sick. The debilitating symptoms of diarrhea and vomiting would have been bad enough if enemy snipers and cleverly booby-trapped minefields hadn't been even more dangerous.

Each night, a few brave soldiers would swim back to the battleship anchored two miles offshore to get more ammunition and supplies. Many never made it back.

In the middle of this sad, miserable jungle, George fought side-by-side with his band of brothers. While others became feverishly sick with dysentery, he raised morale with his wit and charisma. And for a while, things seemed to be getting better. The enemy was being pushed back, and the team was alive.

And then things got tough for George. He became ill. Very ill. Lying in a ditch some might generously call a foxhole, he was so sick he could barely move. With rockets flying overhead and mortars exploding nearby, it was only a matter of time until one landed too close. George wondered how much longer he had to live.

And then it happened.

George and his buddy heard the tell-tale whistle of the incoming mortar. But in their exceptionally weakened state, they didn't have time to move. The round crashed into the back of the foxhole where George's buddy sat huddled. The mortar completely obliterated him, and shrapnel gouged deep flesh out of George's back, buttocks and legs.

For two days George lay in that ditch, with the remains of his dead buddy still covering him. Blood from his gaping wounds mixed with diarrhea and infection set in.

He was a disgusting mess of a soldier. And he was dying.

Despite the pain, George was clear about one thing: to live, he had to get back to the ship. And he would have to get there on his own – there was no one to help him. From the ditch to the beach, and the beach to the boat. They were almost impossible odds for anyone, let alone a man in his pitiful condition. But there was no other option.

And so, when darkness fell, George pulled his wounded body out of the ditch and across the battlefield toward the beach. Using his elbows, he crawled inch by inch by inch. Across the ground still hot from spent artillery shells. Across the bodies of his fallen brothers. His wounds opening fresh with each movement.

Eventually, he made it to the beach. As he crawled into the water, the shock took his breath away. Saltwater burned deep into open, raw wounds – wounds so deep the bones were exposed. The pain was unimaginable, lessened only by a sudden, terrifying thought: What if he couldn't find the boat in the pitch black sea?

Back in Kansas, George had been a state YMCA swimming champion. But that was when he was healthy. He was hardly in any condition to swim a couple of miles to where the support boat was supposed to be waiting. Could he find his way in the darkness...and did he have the strength to make it?

Leaving a trail of blood in the water, he willed himself to move one arm and then the other, his legs too torn up to kick. Stroke after stroke, with life hanging in the balance, George kept swimming. Each movement excruciatingly painful. Each moment deeply traumatic. The minutes turned into hours. And then, far off in the distance, George caught a faint glimpse of the outline of the American boat.

After being pulled from the sea, he collapsed into the arms of shocked medical staff. The doctors, having little hope, focused on making sure he was comfortable in his final hours. For days he lay near death in the infirmary as his body fought infection.

But George didn't die. He was tougher than that. And each day, he got a little bit better.

In spite of the incredible odds, George made it. He lived. And he made it back home to Kansas.

How do you explain that? How do you describe something so primal, so seemingly impossible?

It was blinding fever, diarrhea, deep wounds, burning saltwater and two miles of open ocean versus a ravenous determination to live.

What kept George alive is the same thing that will help you dominate: extreme behavior.

See, it's really quite simple.

The whole discussion about success really comes down to a series of decisions. The first is, are you willing to commit to extreme behavior or will you justify your mediocrity?

Sometimes these things are that simple.

And while that choice seems hard, there is a clarity that comes with the decision.

When you decide that it's going to be hard, when you know that you have to out-work, out-think, out-play and out-muscle everything you do from this day forward, extreme behavior actually becomes a great way to focus what you do.

You have a single-minded purpose – extreme behavior.

And that might be a concept that's hard for you to accept. It goes against everything you probably learned for your advanced business-school degree.

It's socially fashionable to want to "think" your way to the big success that you envision for yourself.

And in some cases that is possible. Combine a decent plan, the right timing and a little bit of luck with reasonable amounts of activity, and you have a chance for big success.

But that formula usually ends up in failure because it represents reasonable amounts of average, mediocre behavior.

In the real world, average strokes are losing strokes.

In the hustle of day-to-day life, a little step forward is really a giant leap backwards.

Small gestures have no place in outrageous success. It's time to stop the nonsense around what it takes to create something amazing.

It takes massive amounts of focused intensity to make the changes that will catapult you to the next level.

It takes extreme behavior.

Extreme behavior manifests in a lot of different ways:

Extreme **effort**.

Extreme **differentiation**.

Extreme **dedication to learning**.

Extreme **discipline**.

Extreme **leadership**.

Extreme **plans**.

Extreme **kindness**.

Extreme **wonder**.

Extreme **beliefs**.

Extreme **patience**.

Extreme **positioning**.

And the list goes on and on. Which ones should you do?

How about all of them?

But start with extreme effort, extreme differentiation and extreme dedication to learning. You can't go wrong being extreme in these three areas.

I can hear you now: "But Dan, isn't extreme behavior the opposite of being balanced?"

Yes it is. I'm glad you pointed that out.

Stop trying to be a balanced person.

Balance doesn't work. It's fairytale unicorn dust sold by "life coaches" to guilt you into thinking that you need to figure out a way to be a little bit of everything.

Nothing could be further from the truth. That's not real.

The best part about a seesaw is that it goes up and down, not that it stays level.

Harmony.
That's what you want to achieve.

Harmony among the various aspects of your life. Not balance. Balance avoids the extremes. And the extremes are where you find real breakthroughs.

Thomas Edison wasn't considered "balanced" when he spent 18 months analyzing more than 10,000 filament combinations to build a working light bulb. And yet that focus led to monumental success.

Being balanced would have meant no light bulb. And a million other equally incredible breakthroughs achieved by unrelenting inventors.

Harmony lets the extremes add perspective and clarity to the boring grit of the daily grind.

Being balanced limits your ability to be amazing. Don't even try to go there.

Look to the edges. Be extreme. Be extreme in everything you do.

And eventually, extreme behavior will become not what you do but who you are.

A winner. Not a whiner.

Tired, sore and wanting to give up.

But refusing to accept anything less than beyond the limits of your capabilities.

Pay the price and you'll find that what you bought was priceless.

George did.

EXTREME **EFFORT**

"Dude, you're just lazy."

Not you. That was me responding to an executive, about 35 minutes into a boring explanation about why he couldn't pivot his business in the right direction.

I did apologize. As extreme as I am, I try to be kind. But it was true, and it just burst right out of my mouth.

Laziness is something I have been noticing more and more of these last few years, in every corner of the world.

Despite the fear, the loss and the uncertainty from the worst economic period in 80 years, it seems that we are doing less than ever. That lack of effort just doesn't add up.

Were we always this content to fail? And then whine about it as if success has nothing to do with the amount of effort that we invest? I don't think so.

My great-grandparents sold matchsticks for a penny a piece during the Great Depression, when a loaf of bread cost about a dime. They were out of work at their factories and yet fought with every ounce of effort to realize their dreams.

It was a culture of effort back then.

And I miss that culture sometimes. Great minds help us do great things. But we actually have to *do* something.

Don't get me wrong – we aren't doing nothing. We have jobs (usually), maybe a business, and a fancy title or two. Our LinkedIn profile is well-scripted and our business card is slick.

But when you cut through all the fluff, here's what I have come to realize:

We aren't doing enough.

Sometimes not even the bare minimum.

But it's even worse than that.

This lack of effort is poor, lazy behavior. In every sense of the words.

I'm not even sure how we got to this point, but here is what I do know:

We talk ourselves out of action before we even get started.

We spend time, mental energy and emotion trying to look good rather than getting results.

We debate the plan rather than working on it.

We make excuses for our mediocrity.

If we want to be successful, it takes doing *more*. A lot more.

To achieve something outrageously extraordinary requires extreme effort.

Lips blue and hands shaking beyond control, Carl Brashear struggled to find the next step up the metal ladder on the side of the pier. Finally, he made it to the top and staggered toward a bench. But beneath the weight of a 200-pound brass diving suit, his legs were no longer strong enough to hold him. He collapsed, barely conscious.

No one had survived this long. No one had ever faced such opposition and made it out alive. For the past nine hours, Carl had searched the ocean floor for the couplings, brackets and screws he needed to complete his task – the arduous, underwater test required to make it into the U.S. Navy's deep-diving corps.

But no one wanted him to pass. It was 1954 and he was a black man fighting to join an all-white, special-forces team. Nothing about the test he faced was fair. While other divers had their parts and tools lowered to them underwater in a sealed canvas bag, Carl's bag was empty. His parts and tools were tossed into the water where they quickly scattered over the ocean floor. To find all the parts and then finish the task was impossible. At least that's what others thought.

Hours after the other divers returned to the surface, Carl fought on. Against supernatural odds and direct opposition from the harsh, underwater world around him, he found deep within himself the power to continue.

Years later, when asked why he fought so hard, he simply stated: "I wasn't going to let nobody steal my dream."

Carl didn't. And neither should you.

Here's the simple truth that Carl Brashear understood all too unfairly:

Effort is the great equalizer.

Seth Godin says ever so brilliantly the following about effort: "People really want to believe effort is a myth.... I think we've been tricked by the veneer of lucky people on the top of the heap. We see the folks who manage to skate by, or who get so much more than we think they deserve, and it's easy to forget that **these guys are the exceptions.... For everyone else, effort is directly related to success....** And that's the key to the paradox of effort: While luck may be more appealing than effort, you don't get to choose luck. **Effort, on the other hand, is totally available, all the time**."

It's inescapable. Effort makes the difference.

Effort is more than "if you pay me more, I'll work harder." It's about not cheating yourself out of your own potential.

Think about that for a minute. Does anyone else really care if you are only putting in a half-ass effort?

NO!

You know deep down you are cheating yourself. And you are the only one who is really hurt by your actions.

No one cares about you like you. The least you can do for yourself is to put in the effort to give your dreams the chance to come true.

Think about what you want out of life right now. Perhaps you want:

More self-assurance about your financial future;

A better relationship with your spouse and children;

A happier and/or more fulfilling lifestyle.

Are you willing to put in the **effort** to make these a reality?

Not brains or money or manipulation. EFFORT!

If all that seems too overwhelming, if your dreams and goals seem too far off, let me offer the simplest of insights:

Effort is simply you taking the next step.

Again and again and again.

When you look closely at how ordinary people achieve amazing things, you begin to see it for what it is: one foot in front of the other. That's all.

A step is infinitely easier than a journey.

It's your decision to be amazing. It's a commitment to take the next step. It's an attitude. It's how you live your life.

Relentlessly moving forward.

The world is full of good people doing good things in good ways. What will change the world is you putting in enough effort to do great things.

One step at a time.

BE EDGY
PUT IN EXTREME EFFORT

1 **Avoid the need to blame others for anything.** Mean, small-minded people know that they suck. That's why they are so cranky and eager to point out others' mistakes. They hope that by causing others to feel inadequate, everyone will forget about how woefully off the mark their own performance is. Don't blame anyone, for any reason, ever. It's a bad habit.

2 **Stop working on things that just don't matter.** Not everything needs to be done in place of sleep. If you work for a boss, then you owe them solid time. You can't cut that out. You can, however, cut out television time, meetings and anything else that gets in the way of achieving your goals. Replace entertainment with activity toward your goal.

3 **Refuse to let yourself wallow in self-doubt. You're alive to succeed.** Stop comparing your current problems to your last 18 failures. They are not the same. You are not the same. Here's something to remember: Your entire life has been a training ground for you to capture your destiny right now. Why would you doubt that? Stop whining. Go conquer.

4 **Ask yourself, "What can I do better next time?" And then do it next time.** If you spend a decade or two earnestly trying to be better, that's exactly what will happen. The next best thing to doing something amazing is not doing something stupid. So learn from your mistakes and use the lessons to dominate.

5 **Proactively take time to do things that fuel your passion** (for example, exercise). Living in the moment requires you to live at peak performance. A huge part of mental fitness is physical fitness. So go fight someone. Or go running if fighting seems a bit extreme. Physical activity accelerates mental motivation.

6 **Apologize to yourself and those around you for having a bad attitude.** Do this once or twice, and you'll snap out of your funk pretty fast. When you start genuinely apologizing for being a bad influence on those around you, you learn to stop whining and start winning.

EXTREME
DIFFERENTIATION

To make a difference, you first must **be** different.

You can't inspire and challenge others when you are just as fearful as they are about standing out and being noticed. Afraid to put yourself in a position where people disagree with you. Afraid to challenge convention. Afraid to be criticized.

Being different is in itself success. Why? Because most of us have a hard time being different.

Standing tall on the trophy stage is pretty easy. But standing up to the rest of the world as an outsider or as a bearer of an original idea requires a lot of effort.

It requires being a mental ninja.

That probably explains why we all aren't more successful.

And here's an observation for you: It's not entirely your fault that you have this fear of being different. Everything you've been taught from the beginning of "baby-dom" was about fitting in.

As you entered school, you were told to "get along with everyone," even when you saw bad people taking advantage of those around you. As long as they didn't mess with you, that was "cool."

When you went out in public, you were told that it was embarrassing to "make a scene" – even though you thought you were standing up for something. You were expressing yourself. But that's how you get shot down, right?

At your first job interview, the HR team asked if you were a team player. And then went on to explain that your compensation was based on individual achievement.

All these "fitting in" qualities produce high-quality mediocrity – a guaranteed batch of Grade-A status quo.

But those qualities don't produce real success – the deeply inspiring breakthroughs that we all dream about.

Real success is the opposite of being like everyone else.

Don't copy what others are doing and thinking. You'll conquer more – and be truer to yourself – when you put in

43

the emotional investment to be different.

It's your obsessive compulsions, your passions, the things that set you apart that produce breakthroughs, not your talent to "fit in."

And you know what?

Being different isn't all that bad.

Being different won't kill you. And it might get you noticed.

Being different probably won't get you incremental job promotions. It's likely to get you something much more.

Being different won't cause people to publicly laud you. At least not at first. But secretly they will respect you.

Being different is about deciding that being like anyone you know – or being your same self – is no longer acceptable.

Frankly, being successful is hard all by itself. Being successful without being different is even harder. Almost impossible.

And extreme behavior is one of the strongest differentiators.

When Jerry Rice entered the NFL in 1985, only two teams were interested in speaking with him. His apparent lack of speed troubled a lot of the scouts evaluating the players. He didn't have the flashiness of the other receivers in the draft. And the college he had played at, Mississippi Valley State University, wasn't a top-tier school. The scouts agreed that Rice was good; but was he good enough for the big leagues?

The San Francisco 49ers decided to take a gamble on Rice and traded picks with the New England Patriots to get him on the team. And Rice didn't disappoint. In fact, he was named the NFC Offensive Rookie of the Year.

But Jerry wanted to be more than a good receiver. He wanted to be extraordinary. The problem was that he made too many mistakes. He dropped too many balls. He felt sluggish and was often hurt.

So he decided to take things up a notch. While other players relaxed during the off-season, Rice brutally trained for hours a day to stay in top physical condition. Most famously, he ran hills. Every day, he ran the trails near his house on a 2.5-mile route that was mostly uphill. A harsh hill. And he did it at a sprinter's pace. Day after day. Grinding through the pain.

When he showed up at training camp that year, four days early, he was in the top physical shape that would define the rest of his Hall-of-Fame career.

Two years later, he led the NFL in touchdown receptions with a number that was twice what anyone else in the league had accomplished. Over the next 20 years, he went on to break or create just about every wide-receiver record on the books. Even at the end of his NFL career, Jerry was one of the fastest and most competitive wide receivers in the game, against defenders who were 15 to 20 years younger than him. Today, Jerry Rice is widely considered the greatest wide receiver of all time, and one of the greatest football players ever to play the game.

Jerry Rice was naturally talented. But so were dozens of other football players who played beside him.

He had "good instincts." But so did hundreds of other players in the NFL.

Jerry differentiated himself from all the other players in the league through extreme behavior. He was willing to push the limits.

You probably don't need to be running brutal hills every day like Jerry Rice. But you need to be different.

Being different
makes the difference.

And it's not about just doing something better than anyone else.

It's about pushing the limits. And I don't mean pushing the limits just a little.

Extreme differentiation means pushing the limits a little further than anyone else ever dares to.

It means understanding that the only limits that exist are the ones in your head.

You might be thinking that your boss or your company sets the limits. They don't.

You might be thinking that your spouse or your family sets the limits. They don't.

You set the limits.

Which is why to be successful you need to push your limits.

What stands in your way of greatness isn't challenges or obstacles or your perceived limitations. What stands in your way is the misguided belief that what you want to do is impossible.

Push your limits and you'll realize that "impossible" really isn't impossible after all.

Maybe it's time for new limits. Or no limits at all.

That's for you to decide.

Pushing your limits is the ultimate differentiator.

And being different positions you to change the world.

Start being different today.

BE EDGY
5 WAYS TO PUSH YOUR LIMITS

1 **Understand the fears that drive you.** Pushing your limits starts with an awareness of what really drives you – the scary stuff that you're afraid to admit. You are most successful when you look your demons in the eye and admit your weaknesses.

2 **Demand extra effort from yourself, even when it doesn't seem possible.** You might think you're giving 100%, but that's not likely. Frankly, it's not even possible. It's pure fantasy. Putting in the extra effort is about you doing that one more thing that needs to be done. It's about the pain you're willing to endure until you get what you want.

3 **Stop worrying about what other people think of you.** Someone else's opinion is the number one reason you're going to fail. Are you willing to trade your future for some idiot with a loud mouth? It's silly how obsessed we are with what others think about us. Instead of trying to look like you're amazing, how about just being amazing?

4 **Deliberately place yourself in challenging situations where failure seems likely.** Anybody can be a winner when it's easy. That's not a challenge. But that's what most of us do – we win when it's easy. If you want to push your limits, you need to sign up for failure. You need to boldly gamble on yourself. Sometimes being backed into a corner is the motivation you need to be successful.

5 **Question everything.** Just because "it" is, doesn't mean that's the way "it" should be or could be. It just means that's the way it is right now. Pushing your limits means that you look facts in the face and discredit them. You challenge reality. You refuse to believe that your will is weaker than the way things are right now.

EXTREME
DEDICATION TO
LEARNING

Pretending that we know more than we really do is one big reason we're not as successful as we should be. It's probably the worst self-limiting behavior that we have.

What is especially challenging about this bad habit is that our culture pressures us to believe that we should know everything about anything...that to be at the top of our game, we have to be all-knowing. Always be right. Never make a mistake.

Of course, knowing everything is just not possible. And to pretend otherwise is not healthy. It's just stupid.

Yet we all do it – act like we have it all together out of some false need to protect ourselves or our vulnerabilities.

Instead of pursuing answers, we spend our time pretending like we already have the answers.

Frankly, that kind of attitude and those actions come from fear – fear of being seen as ignorant or limited or small.

And that fear keeps you from being amazing.

It keeps you from taking advantage of the opportunities around you.

It limits your ability to master new things.

It is the reason you don't read more and better educate yourself.

It limits your creativity to explore new ideas.

It keeps you from seeing the world outside your own prejudices.

It prevents you from complimenting successes that aren't your own.

It alienates people who would otherwise help you.

At some point you have to look past your fear of "not knowing" and just live the life that you really want for yourself.

Why pretend to know when you can create a habit of knowing?

Why pose when you can empower?

In fact, if it's a contest between *looking* like you know and *really* knowing...well, that's not a contest at all, is it?

Related to the belief that you have to know everything is the belief that you are always right.

It's a mindset that is crippling on a lot of levels.

Let's dig into the psychology of this.

You're not always right. But you already know that. (You do know that, right?)

And it's not a secret – even though you work overtime hoping no one around you finds out.

Which is silly. Because they already know that you're flawed.

And they know that you know that you're flawed – which is both frustrating and confusing.

Despite your bravado and charm, they know you make mistakes.

Which would be okay, if you actually stopped to apologize. To admit being wrong.

Which begs another question: Why do we find it so difficult to be wrong? (How much do you want to bet it has something to do with fear?)

Here's a simple thought for you:

There is power in being wrong.

A big part of success is humility – the belief that you always have more to learn.

But if you're always right, there is never a need to learn more.

Perhaps the biggest wrong is in thinking that you are always right.

"That'll never work...."

Those are the first words you hear coming out of your mouth.

You have a plan and you're pushing forward, but if anyone suggests some change or a different idea, you immediately kick in with that defensive stance.

Admit it...you've been there before. We all have.

But when you say something won't work, you allow your brain to kick into its fear pattern.

Your natural reaction is to dig in your heels rather than having the flexibility to consider, "Hmm...maybe so. Let's look at that."

The trap is in being defensive.

Defensive reactions keep you from being the all-star that you really want to be – that you really can be. And you're not even really sure why you're defensive.

With a simple, "That'll never work," you've stopped learning. You've stopped moving forward.

But let's think about this for a minute. You don't really know that what you just heard won't work, right?

You probably haven't tested your theory eight ways to Sunday in a secret underground laboratory.

You haven't visited the Library of Congress to read every book known to man on that particular topic.

There's no evidence to prove whether the idea will work or not.

The truth is, you haven't given the idea more than two seconds of thought. And yet you have an opinion. And a particularly strong one at that!

Here's why: You don't like new ideas.

That's actually normal. If it's new, it's scary. That's how the human brain is wired. And it kept our ancestors alive, when wandering too far from the village might mean stumbling into a hungry saber-toothed tiger.

But that defensive attitude might be costing you high performance.

When faced with something new, you can do what comes naturally and be defensive. Or you can commit to curiosity and learning.

The secret is having an extreme obsession with figuring it all out.

When you dedicate yourself to a life of pursuing answers, amazing things happen.

In 1869, John Roebling began work on a suspension bridge that would connect Manhattan to Brooklyn for the first time (known today as the Brooklyn Bridge). It was a project that would take more than 13 years to complete and cost the lives of almost 30 workers.

Nothing like this had ever been done before. It was a massive feat of engineering complexity – the first steel-wire suspension bridge, and for more than 20 years, the longest suspension bridge in the world. For five years ahead of the launch, John and his team worked tirelessly. Without the aid of computer systems, he created new ways to explore under water and measure the bedrock in order to place the foundation pillars in key locations.

But John didn't live long enough to see the completion of the bridge. Just three days after construction began, he was working on the edge of a dock when an arriving ferry crushed the toes on his right foot. He requested that his toes be amputated so that he could continue working on the bridge. Tetanus took his life a few weeks later.

Having learned the science and art of bridge building from his father, Washington Roebling took over the project as Chief Engineer. However, just a few months later, he suffered a crippling underwater accident that left him with shattered health and made him an invalid for the rest of his life.

But Washington was the only one with the knowledge to keep the project on track. So, as he lay in bed far away from the construction site, he taught his wife, Emily, higher mathematics, stress analysis, materials strength and the fine details of steel-cable construction. As the liaison between Washington and the engineers onsite, Emily became the first woman field engineer.

At times, Washington became so sick that he lost the ability to speak. Not to be deterred, he taught himself Morse code and tapped out instructions on Emily's arm. Every step, every day, he slowly but determinedly tapped his way to success.

Washington and Emily spent the next 11 years working together to build the bridge – Washington from his bed – while politicians, engineers and competing companies tried to steal his project and the spotlight. Husband and wife learned their way around politics, technology and Washington's impairments until the bridge was finally completed. On May 24, 1883, Emily was the first person to walk across the bridge. Washington was too sick to attend.

At the opening ceremony, Emily was honored in a speech by Abram Hewitt who said the bridge was "...an everlasting monument to the sacrificing devotion of a woman and of her capacity for that higher education from which she has been too long disbarred." And of Washington's conducting the largest and most difficult engineering project to date, it was said: "Nowhere in the history of great undertakings is there anything comparable."

One hundred and thirty years later, the Brooklyn Bridge is still in use and an icon of New York City. More than 120,000 vehicles, 4,000 pedestrians and 2,600 cyclists cross the bridge every day. Following several New York City blackouts and the 9-11 attacks on the World Trade Center, tens of thousands of people used the bridge to escape Manhattan.

The Roeblings could not have foreseen the unique stresses on the bridge from the massive numbers of people that would one day cross it on foot, yet they designed it with three separate systems to handle unanticipated structural stresses. John Roebling famously said that if anything happened to one of the systems, "The bridge may sag, but it will not fall."

And if that wasn't as staggeringly successful as one family might attempt, Washington Roebling didn't stop there. He set out to learn biology, and that quest consumed the next 43 years of his life as he collected rocks and minerals from all over the world. Today, his scientific collection of over 16,000 specimens is an important part of the Smithsonian Institute.

The Roeblings were a family who simply never stopped learning.

In the face of tragedies and hardships, they made no excuses. They got kicked in the teeth over and over again and made the decision to keep going and figure it out anyway.

They accomplished extraordinary success because of their outrageous dedication to learning and their relentless drive to discover what they didn't know.

Yes, it might seem extreme. An extreme dedication to learning is not a "vanilla pudding" life strategy.

But being maniacally dedicated to learning new things might just be the single biggest factor in you accomplishing outrageous acts of super-stardom.

So let's get practical.

Learning is not some magical happenstance that falls all around you.

Learning is about **capturing the lessons that are happening all around you.**

That doesn't happen automatically. Or else we would all be learning the lessons that could make us extraordinary.

It takes massive and relentless focus on becoming a learner. And that means going out of your way to make life your laboratory.

You don't wait for answers to magically appear. You actively look for answers from everything around you.

You don't learn only when you feel like it. And you don't learn only the lessons that you want to learn.

Being *willing* to learn is different from *hoping* you will learn something.

Being a learner means taking what life serves you – fair or not – and turning it into either the best choice or some kind of understanding. It's using the worst moments in life to plan your future best moments.

And sometimes, you need to learn the same lesson a few different ways.

We all like to think that when presented with the right facts, we learn the right lessons the first time around. Sadly, that's not usually how it works.

It's okay (and perfectly normal) to be a little "thick" at times. The key is to keep learning. Even if it means learning the same lesson over and over again.

Learning is also about curiosity, about purposefully putting yourself in the position to find answers to your questions.

It's about asking questions until you know, until you really have clarity, so that you can be the best "you" possible.

Here are a few questions that work:

"Tell me more...."

"I'm not sure I understand...."

"What makes you say that?"

"Can you clarify what you mean?"

Regardless of the exact words you say, you need to keep asking until you understand.

Sure, at times you might feel like a fool with non-stop questions. But your feelings on the subject aren't really that important if what you want is outrageous success.

You need to be learning. You probably already agree with that.

But here's the real question for you:

Are you learning? *Are* you obsessed with figuring it out?

The other option is to be a loser – stuck, silent and scared.

And that clearly sounds like the worse of the two options.

The way to win is to keep seeking knowledge. No one can stop you when you refuse to stop looking for answers.

BE EDGY
MAKE LIFE YOUR LABORATORY

1. Take notes while reading a book.

2. Be a mentor.

3. Get a mentor and ask what you can do better.

4. Listen to contrarian points of view.

5. Put out a risky question in a crowded room.

6. Reach out for help when life gets tough.

7. Write down the last 5 reasons you failed.

8. Stop saying "uh-huh" and "yeah" when you don't know.

9. Be grateful for unexpected lessons.

10. Keep a running list of books you want to read – and start reading.

11. Keep asking "Why?"

12. Share key knowledge that you have acquired.

13. Take 3 new friends to coffee and learn from their talents.

14. Stop watching so much television.

15. Tour a museum and take a few pictures.

16. Put together a list of lessons you've learned.

17. Read the *USA Today* newspaper or the *Wall Street Journal*.

18. Adapt new vocabulary into everyday conversation.

19. Stop tweeting; start reading.

20. Be kind when you know something that someone else doesn't know.

21. Be involved in music, sports or a hobby.

22. Push your body to the limits with exercise and activity.

DISCIPLINED ACTIVITY

Make no mistake. Just putting in mind-bending amounts of
raw effort isn't enough to make you successful.

You will get some things done. And perhaps the right
things will get done.

But success isn't that simple.

It requires more than that.

It requires discipline.

You see, you won't be successful overnight. You won't.

Stop thinking that success is a sprint. It's not.

Progress takes time. And it takes discipline to keep you focused until you get there.

It's no wonder that being successful is the subject of countless books, articles and self-help seminars. It's hard to do.

And yet, in spite of all the training and expertise about how to be successful, we seem to lack interest in the most guaranteed way to realize outrageous success: disciplined activity.

Growing up as the second of five children, I was raised by parents who understood the art of disciplined practice and relentlessly demanded it. Starting from the age of five, each of us was required to practice the piano at least one hour per day. That increased to two hours per day as we grew older and our lessons became more taxing.

But it wasn't just an hour for the piano. It was an hour for each instrument we played, and all of us played several. I played the euphonium (a smaller, more eloquent tuba) and the trombone. Why the euphonium? Because no one had ever heard of it before. I practiced in the basement, for hours at a time, until my lips would go numb, and I'd have to stop for a few minutes. And the practice paid off – I became an accomplished national prep-school competitor. It wasn't that I was naturally talented. Hardly. The forced discipline produced success.

But that success wasn't enough. I can remember the feeling of wanting more, a passion for outrageous success boiling under the surface. You see, right around the time that I was winning awards for brass, my older brother was equally tearing up the piano scene. This also was about the same time that I decided I was done with the piano. And my parents were okay with that. Suddenly, I got back an hour of my life every day.

But a strange thing happened. I found myself returning to the piano from time to time. I played just for the joy of it, really hearing the keys as they touched the wires, feeling the pressure of the pads as my fingers trickled over the keys. And then one day it hit me: I wanted back in. I wanted to create art with the piano.

So I mentioned to my mother that I was thinking about starting piano lessons again and competing in the state classical music competition the following year. To which she replied, "Oh, that's okay. You're good at brass. Let your brother be good at that." She never said it and didn't intend it, but what I heard was, "You're not good enough." At that moment, I knew that I wanted to prove her wrong more than anything else in the world. And that became my mission.

And so I began the first of hundreds of hours of deliberate practice. My goal was to play Rachmaninoff's "Opus 3, Number 2" perfectly. I practiced for hours – after school, on the weekends, in the evenings. Ten fingers in C# Minor, and I was using each one of them.

Once I learned the notes, I learned to feel them. The way you leave your fingers on the edge of the keys for a half-second as the music reverberates off the soundboard. The silky-smooth transition between the racing scales in the second movement. The way to pause ever so slightly before the fastest parts to pull the listener into the experience.

Months later, I heard my name being called to take the stage at the competition. And then I did what I had done hundreds of times before. I felt the music – the tone, the shape, the sounds. And it moved me. It moved the judges, too. As I finished and stood up, I noticed that three of the judges had tears in their eyes. I found out several hours later that I had won.

That experience taught me a powerful lesson about the art of discipline and practicing my way to outrageous success.

That is when I learned that with discipline and enough effort, I could do just about anything.

The rewards of discipline and effort are vast.

You just need to get started.

And then persist.

It takes guts to put in the practice and preparation to stick with your dreams when there is a possibility you might not achieve them, right? At least when those around you think you won't achieve them.

Let's be candid. That's hard work.

It's the ultimate in deferred gratification, which is hard for most of us.

Not one of us would expect to be able to play Mozart's "Symphony #41 in C Major" on the piano the first time we try. We understand that it takes thousands of hours of deliberate practice to successfully play a concert-level concerto.

But for some reason we get frustrated when we can't master our wildest dreams in a single six-week spurt. We become frustrated when we try something a few times and don't get immediate results.

Amazing things rarely happen quickly or the first time you try. In fact, they rarely happen the first few hundred times you try.

And that is exactly why you need discipline – to give yourself the chance to do something amazing.

THE DISCIPLINE OF **DOING**

According to multiple studies, the average age of a successful entrepreneur is mid-40s.

That got me thinking: "How many more years do I have before I get to the finish line and achieve my goals?"

I'm 33 right now. At my age, French Egyptologist Jean-François Champollion deciphered the Rosetta Stone, British physician Thomas Wedgwood produced the first photograph and Gregory Pincus achieved in-vitro fertilization of rabbits. Mind-blowing feats of genius.

But the odds indicate that I probably have a decade of mind-blowing effort ahead of me before I do something amazing. Another ten years of waking up each morning and going the distance.

Maybe you do, too.

So, if that's the case – that you and I have to go the distance – it's important to get serious about the race.

The race for success is long.

The race is tough.

Your legs get tired. You get thirsty. Every fiber of your being wants to throw in the towel and call it quits.

And yet your best chance at success – at winning the race – is to hang in there. To keep going. To keep *doing*.

Guys like Cliff Young show us how it's done.

Albert Ernest Clifford Young died in 2003 at the age of 81. Twenty years earlier, at a spry 61 years of age, the Australian potato farmer accomplished the impossible: He beat all the other runners at the Melbourne Ultra-Marathon.

The race started in Sydney and ended 875 kilometers (544 miles) away in Melbourne. Surrounded by elite athletes from all over the world, Cliff showed up at the starting line in gumboots and a pair of soiled overalls. He was more than 40 years older than some of his competitors.

As the race started and the other runners began executing their racing strategies, Cliff shuffled along at a slow, awkward pace. He quickly fell to the back of the pack of runners, where he remained for some time. And then something amazing happened.

Cliff just kept running.

While the other runners stopped to sleep, he shuffled along. Five days, 15 hours and four minutes later, Cliff crossed the finish line. It wasn't even close. He had broken the record by almost two full days.

Cliff Young refused to let age, fatigue or lack of proper gear get in the way of his will to win.

Now don't shoot the messenger here, but the odds are that you will quit before you win the race. (The odds are scary.) Because it's all too easy to do what feels good *right now*.

But the comfort of quitting is not worth the prize you will be giving up.

Maybe you will only give up temporarily. Just stop for a rest, take a quick break. Then get back in the race.

Maybe you won't.

Maybe you will become like everyone else around you – the wishful thinkers who give up and later ask themselves, "What if...?"

What if you choose instead to discipline yourself and go the distance?

Going the distance takes an unflinching commitment and a passionate emotional investment in your long-term success. Passion is the antidote to the setbacks you will surely face on the way to success.

It's that often-illogical passion and emotion that allows you to keep going long after it makes sense.

When you put enough of yourself into something, you will do whatever it takes to make sure you come out on the winning end of things. But when you jump into a quick "emotional fling," you have so little invested that it's easy to give up on yourself.

Ultimately, it comes down to your ability to fight through the pain long after the race stops being "fun."

And don't plan on getting a break any time soon.

You have to keep pushing forward without any guarantee of when you can stop. The key is in not expecting to catch a break.

That's why you need the discipline to stay focused and keep *doing*.

That's why you have to make continuous progress.

The concept of continuous progress is not groundbreaking in originality and certainly not trendy enough to be found in

Harvard Business Review. But it is exactly what you need to realize your dreams.

The only thing standing between you and outrageous success is continuous progress.

Stopping and starting causes massive damage – emotional and physical.

Steady progress is the key to success. A long race is just a series of smaller steps.

Disciplined action builds momentum.

By leveraging small but continuous progress, you take a series of meaningful steps toward what might otherwise be an unattainable goal.

Continuous *doing* is the secret.

You're still around after everyone else has given up.

When they are gasping for air, you are pumping your legs and pushing for the finish line.

A lot of life comes down to doing hard things when you least feel like it.

If you're going to be successful over the long run, you're going to have to do things that hurt on days when you already hurt.

Which seems to defy logic. If you're already not at peak performance, it might seem like a better option to recuperate and then get back in the race.

That's what most of us have been taught to do since we were children. If we weren't feeling well, we didn't have to go to school. If we got hurt, we took it easy for a while.

So it's only natural that you might think you can be

successful while living life on easy terms. And not just "easy" terms...your terms.

But the reality of success is that to get what you want from life, you're going to have to gut it out.

At work, in relationships, in life, there are days when it's not so easy to do the right thing.

Maybe you try to justify not doing anything by rationalizing that you'll start doing better when you feel better. When the terms for success are better.

But anyone can play the game and do pretty well when the odds are in their favor. Anyone can conquer when the opponent doesn't have a weapon.

The challenge is to do what is hard and noble and right when you are sick and tired, and tired and sick. When you don't feel like doing anything at all.

For 22 years, Joannie Rochette had trained to be in this position. She had practiced and practiced, turning her 17th-place showing at the World Figure Skating Championship into second place five years later. Along the way, she had competed in 39 competitions and picked up international medals in China, Russia and at the Grand Prix. Now, she was entering the 2010 Winter Olympics in Vancouver as the reigning world silver medalist and six-time Canadian champion. Expectations for her were high as Canada's best chance to win an Olympic figure-skating medal.

The stage was set.

Two days before she was scheduled to compete, just as she was beginning her final practice, she was startled by a surprise visit from her father. He told Joannie that her mother, Thérèse, had just died from a massive heart attack. The news was shocking and devastating. Everything she had ever worked for seemed to leave her soul as the tears flowed from her eyes. What deep sorrow. How could she continue?

Fast forward two days. As Joannie took the ice, the crowd was quiet. This was their hometown girl. Not sure whether to cry with her or to cheer her on to victory, they waited.

As the opening notes of "La Cumparsita" filled the arena, Joannie moved to the emotion of the moment – every triple lutz crisp, every combination passionate, as if she were willing herself to win.

When the music was over, Joannie bowed, tears streaming uncontrollably down her face. She had put on the performance of a lifetime. The crowd stood, wildly applauding. They seemed to know that they were part of a special moment – a perfect three minutes of passion, purpose and, yes, pain.

Joannie had but one thing to say: "C'est pour toi, Maman." ("For you, Mom.")

Joannie Rochette won the bronze medal for figure skating, adding Olympic Champion to a long list of awards. She was also chosen as the flag bearer for the closing ceremonies and won the Terry Fox Award as the athlete who most inspired courage and determination at the 2010 Winter Olympics.

You are sadly mistaken if you think you can be successful by taking action only when you feel like it.

There are no sick days.

Get that idea out of your head.

Every day matters.

Today matters. And tomorrow, too.

It takes discipline (and a lot of it) to keep moving forward – to keep *doing* – in spite of the obstacles.

Believe it or not, the past 24 hours of your life have a lot to do with how you feel about your goals, your potential, your stamina and the guts you need to summon to get past the pain to become a success.

And those perceptions can change pretty quickly.

A day from now, how you feel will be completely different.

Discipline forces you to make progress every day regardless of how you feel. You learn to look past the pain and fear of the moment, past your changing perceptions and feelings, and just take another step.

And over time, you realize that your emotions are less important than you doing something.

Disciplined doing is the secret to domination.

Discipline can help you beat the odds, even when they seem stacked against you.

There isn't a lot you have to remember:

Stay in the race.
Keep moving forward.

If you aren't moving forward, you just aren't getting any closer to success. You aren't.

And never forget that the finish line is usually hidden until you're almost upon it.

So run as long as you can run. Then walk until you can no longer walk. And then crawl, pulling yourself by your fingertips until your knuckles cramp up.

But never stop moving toward success.

BE EDGY
FINISH THE RACE

1 **Prepare for the long haul.** Stay in shape mentally, physically and financially. Invest in your dream by thinking about the long-term effects of your activities. If they won't stand the test of time, don't do them.

2 **You can recover from a few falls along the way.** Don't get discouraged by failure. You will get banged up. That's just what happens. But you have to decide that the more you fall, the faster you will get back up. No matter the damage, you will survive. Even from the bad stuff, the unthinkable stuff.

3 **Which next step isn't as important as you simply taking one.** Doing the right thing many times means you just need to do the next thing. Because if you stop doing the right thing before it starts working, you've just done the wrong thing.

4 **Everyone who is in the race is just as tired as you are.** If you're still in the race right now, take a look around. Those people around you are feeling the same pain you are feeling. It's no easier for anyone else. It's not harder for you. It's all about knowing that you're hurting and deciding that you want success more than you want to avoid the pain.

THE DISCIPLINE OF **DENYING**

Most of us are willing to do almost anything in order to realize our goals.

We will turn over any stone, cross any bridge, scale any metaphorical mountain in order to achieve success.

Or at least that's what we say.

We are quick to talk about how disciplined we are. How motivated we keep ourselves. How "on point" and energized we are.

But success often has less to do with what we are willing to do than what we are willing to do *without*.

We tend to think of discipline as a series of tasks that we need to complete in order to achieve success. A few key action items that we need to repeat day after day after day.

But the *doing* part is only one side of discipline. The harder, grittier side of discipline is what you *won't* do.

Discipline is as much about *denying* as it is about *doing*.

And that takes guts. Daily guts.

It's not easy to say "no" to yourself.

It's not easy to talk yourself out of something that makes your life more comfortable now. (Never mind what it might mean in the future.)

And your brain isn't wired to help you.

Of all the massive computing power in your brain, only one little portion is wired to help you deny yourself. Just one part of the brain controls inhibition and the higher reasoning that stops you from doing things.

And it's a highly moody section of the brain.

If you've had too much caffeine, it gets jumpy.

If you haven't eaten or gotten enough sleep, it slows down.

If you've been drinking, it turns off completely.

And it's the only part of your brain stopping you from immediate gratification.

Without discipline – extreme discipline – you give in to your every whim and desire.

Instead of toughing it out, you decide to "let it slide this time." And the next time. And the time after that.

And it becomes harder and harder to deny yourself what you want right now.

You become addicted to immediate gratification.

And every time you give in, you feed that addiction.

But it's not just you.

As a society, we've become addicted to immediate gratification. We say "yes" to everything. We have to have what we want, and we have to have it *right now*.

"It's not fair" if we have to wait or earn something the hard way.

And there is some logic to that. You see, for hundreds of years, each successive generation has been better off than the ones before. But according to recent studies, most of us believe that our children will be worse off than we are.

For the first time in history, we see the future negatively. Economic, cultural and technological shifts have made us fearful that things are not going to get better – that this is as good as it's going to get.

And so there is a strong undercurrent of "I have to get mine and get it now" thinking. Things won't get any better than they are right now, so why shouldn't you get what you want?

But that kind of attitude will cripple you in the long term.

That addiction to immediate gratification is killing your dream.

Addiction is not a good model for inspired living. In fact, it's unbelievably damaging.

So let's talk about it.

Discussions about addiction usually focus on personal vices like gambling or alcohol, drugs or pornography. Addictions that are socially unacceptable. Addictions that have obvious, dramatic and negative effects.

But no one discusses the subtle, seemingly innocuous addictions that rob us of our true potential. We're not good at admitting the ugly side of under-performance:

We're addicted to fear.

We're addicted to making excuses.

We're addicted to passive aggression.

We're addicted to selfishness.

We're addicted to listening to the crowd.

We're addicted to vegging in front of the TV.

We're addicted to the safety a paycheck provides.

We're addicted to comfort.

We're addicted to taking the easy way out.

These are socially acceptable addictions.

Addictions that we let others get away with because we see them in ourselves.

We excuse these addictions as if the frailty of our humanity is a worthy excuse for our inadequacies. *It's not.*

Being human does not demand that you live broken. That you let your weaknesses drive your behavior and determine your future.

Which begs an important question:

What are you addicted to?

It might be hard to admit, but your addictions play a significant role in the decisions you make each day. Your addictions decide whether you relentlessly pursue your goals or give in to how your brain subconsciously makes decisions.

And day by day, month by month, you become more and more lazy about denying your addictions.

Until one day, you are no longer a champion. No longer a warrior.

But you can choose to feed a different addiction.

How about being addicted to greatness?

How about being addicted to *delayed* gratification instead of immediate gratification? How about choosing purpose over comfort?

Your addiction is your decision.

You are mighty because of your ability to choose what is hard over what is easy.

Mike Weaver could be the "poster child" for choosing what is hard over what is easy.

Mike Weaver took up boxing in the swamps of Vietnam in 1970. Not yet 20 years old, the young Marine found the training deeply inspiring and threw himself into it with a fierce passion. After Vietnam, he moved to California where he trained to the point of exhaustion. But his results were lackluster at best.

Rather than sulking about why he wasn't reaping the rewards of his efforts, he denied himself the luxury of giving up. It would have been easier to quit – to concede that he would likely never achieve his dream of becoming a boxing legend. Instead, he pushed himself harder.

And it didn't go unnoticed. He became a favorite sparring partner for Muhammad Ali. Although he lacked finesse, his chiseled physique and incredible strength tested the abilities of the more talented boxers against whom he sparred. That's what he seemed to be good at – making other boxers better. No one believed in him or his dream to be a champion.

For the next half-decade, Weaver languished in obscurity, the "punching bag" of more capable superstars. He blew every lucky break he got, losing six of his first dozen fights. But the experts agreed that he was starting to show promise. Despite his lack of skills, he was able to last longer in each subsequent fight, sometimes just barely losing in the final rounds.

Mike realized that he would have to achieve his dream the hard way. He would have to work even harder to get what he wanted. He stayed disciplined, and he stayed focused. And that commitment was about to pay off.

On March 3, 1980, Mike Weaver walked into the Stokely Athletic Center in Knoxville, TN, to fight the undefeated John Tate for the WBA Heavyweight title. Quite the opposite of Weaver, Tate was a boxing phenom. Initially a star amateur boxer who had fought in the 1976 Olympics, Tate had quickly amassed a 20-0 record as a professional. In sensational form, he had captured the Heavyweight title from Gerrie Coetzee in South Africa in front of 100,000 of Coetzee's fans. Tate was electrifying and charismatic, and the fans adored him.

The fight against Weaver was nothing more than another stepping stone for Tate, another notch in his belt. Tate immediately went to work on Weaver. Fighting 25 pounds heavier than Weaver, he moved effortlessly through the first ten rounds – smashing Weaver with wicked jabs and brutal right hooks.

Weaver had never had to finish a 15-round fight before. He had always finished his fights much earlier, and the fatigue was evident. As the bell for round 15 sounded, Tate glided around the ring, minutes away from victory.

But Weaver pressed the fight. Knowing that his only chance to win was a knockout, he picked up the tempo. He was desperate. After a decade of getting his head punched in, he was fighting in the title match. And he wasn't going to go away quietly. His arms felt like rubber, but he kept swinging. The announcer, ringside, noted that Weaver seemed to fight harder in the 15th round than in the fifth.

With only 40 seconds left in the match, Weaver hit John Tate with a left hook that knocked him out cold. It was the right punch at the right time. It was a punch he had been practicing for 10 years. And it left Tate unconscious on the canvas for minutes.

Against all odds, Mike Weaver became the Heavyweight Champion of the World and one of the greatest boxing inspirations of all time. For 10 years, Weaver denied himself immediate gratification, immediate glory, immediate rewards, immediate recognition. When no one else believed in him, he kept going. He stayed disciplined.

How long could you keep going if you weren't getting the breaks you thought you deserved? Could you deny yourself immediate gratification for 10 years if it meant you could have your dream?

Rise up. Muster the courage to deny yourself what you desire now so you can have your ultimate goal.

You have to proactively say "no" to some things in order to say "yes" to what you really want.

Choose the discipline of denial:

Say "no" to self-limiting behaviors and attitudes.

Say "no" to the need to look like you're right all of the time.

Say "no" to immediate gratification.

Say "no" to feeling good emotionally right now.

Say "no" to playing the victim.

Say "no" to being lazy.

Say "no" to the minutiae that cripples you.

Say "no" to what is easy or natural.

These are incredibly hard things to do. Gut-wrenchingly hard. Even harder to do consistently.

But being successful demands that you make brutally hard decisions each day about what you will and will not do.

You can do a lot of things, but if you don't deny yourself certain things at the same time, your efforts are wasted.

You can work harder and make more money. But if you spend more money than you make, your extra effort is just wasted.

It's not only what you are willing to do that will make you successful; it's also what you are willing to do without until you get there.

What's holding you back is not an advanced college degree, the right connections or more money in the bank.

It's your lack of discipline.

You want someone to hand you a dream. That just isn't going to happen. It's not.

Both doing and denying are integral to success.

So, what are you willing to do without?

DISCIPLINE **STARTS WITH A PLAN**

You will be whatever you are planning to be.

Let that sink in for a moment....

Chances are that you won't win the lottery or have a rich uncle leave you a small fortune. If you are like the majority of people, you will stumble through life making excuses for your failures, trying to stay optimistic that success is right around the corner.

But what if you could guarantee that outrageous success really is right around the corner?

What if you could bank on the EDGY prediction that everything you ever wanted for yourself will happen? That you could make it happen?

Here's a little secret for you:

You can have whatever you want in life as long as you are willing to plan for it.

And then execute, of course.

That is the doing and denying part. On the one hand, you are feverishly focusing on achieving success. On the other, you are toughing it out, purposefully saying "no" to what is easy.

Planning is where discipline starts.

In essence, if you can plan it, you can have it.

Anything.

The bigger your goal, the bigger and badder your plan needs to be. The bigger the reward you expect from success, the riskier your plan has to be.

Lasse Viren tells us that story best.

Lasse Viren of Finland was a police officer who appeared on the international track scene in 1971 running the 5,000-meter and 10,000-meter events. He finished a forgettable seventh and 17th place in each race, respectively. The problem was that he ran too fast at the beginning and then faded fast.

If the story stopped at that point, there would be nothing much to talk about. Lasse looked like a big loser, like every other failed athlete who just didn't try hard enough. But as Lasse finished his second race, while dust and sweat still hung in the air, he started planning his success.

Determined to achieve his goals, Lasse decided to move more than 4,000 miles away to Thompson Falls in Kenya to begin a brutal training regimen. Under the 250-foot scenic waterfall at the base of the Ewaso Narok River, he pushed his body to the breaking point each day. As the mist of the powerful waterfall sprayed around him, he planned to smash the world-record time for a two-mile race at an event in Helsinki, Finland, in the summer of 1972. And he did just that.

Yet his success wasn't complete. Despite the world record, Lasse entered the last half of 1972 as a relative unknown. But his next goal – to dominate at the upcoming Munich Olympics – was audacious. So his plan had to be audacious.

He logged thousands of kilometers running in the local forests back in Finland, sprinting at gradually increasing intensities to prepare for the race of his life. Still not satisfied with his training, he mastered the art of "bend mathematics," where he practiced running along the very inner edge of the first lane. He figured this plan would save him tens of meters over his competitors.

The plan was coming together. But would it be enough for him to be successful?

Lasse headed to the Munich Olympics, and on September 3, 1972, he took his place at the starting line of the

10,000-meter event, ready to take his plan to the finish line. After the gun sounded, Lasse ran to the front of the pack, right behind celebrity runner Steve Prefontaine. And that's where Lasse stayed for the first 12 laps.

Until he fell.

Lasse's legs got entangled with those of the runner from Tunisia, Mohammed Gammoudi, and he crashed to the track – quickly falling to last place, meters behind the fast-moving pack of runners. With desperation fueling every part of his body and soul, Lasse got back on his feet and started running. In less than 150 meters, he caught up with the race leaders. The faster Prefontaine pushed the pace, the faster Lasse ran. He was bruised, panting and wildly determined.

He had planned to win, and this was his chance. With 600 meters left in the race, Lasse began to sprint at a pace no one could match. Leaving everyone, including Prefontaine, in the dust, he crossed the finish line in first place. Lasse's plan helped him win a gold medal and set a new world record.

But his plan for success didn't stop there. You see, Lasse was just getting started.

A week later, he won a gold medal in the 5,000-meter finals, ahead of Prefontaine and a trio of all-star runners. Then just a few days after his Olympic triumphs, in a light drizzle in Helsinki, Lasse amazingly set a new world record in the 5,000-meter race. At the Olympics four years later, Lasse again won gold medals in both the 5,000- and 10,000-meter events, against what some would say were more challenging competitors than those he had faced in Munich.

Lasse Viren, a policeman from Finland, accomplished what no other athlete had ever done or has done since: won back-to-back Olympic gold medals in the 5,000- and 10,000-meter events. It may never be done ever again.

And it was all because he had a plan.

You may think that success comes when you cross the finish line.

But nothing could be further from the truth.

Success comes when you make your plan.

It's all about the plan.

What are you planning right now?

It's a serious question that deserves serious thought.

Know this: You will be whatever you are planning to be.

Let that sink in for a moment.

If what you're planning right now is the success you will see in years to come, how successful will you be?

Will you be happy with the person you are planning to become?

Are you even planning at all?

BE EDGY
PLAN FOR YOUR SUCCESS

1 **Plan to work harder than you ever imagined.** You might not move to Kenya to sweat under the hot sun as you train to break world records, but you may spend a decade of sleepless nights until you make your way to the finish line. And you need to plan for that. Success and "living a balanced life" should not be in the same sentence. It takes extreme effort to be successful, not a 9-to-5 work ethic. You need to plan to work harder than you ever imagined...and then double that effort.

2 **Your plan should be bigger than simply "not losing" – it needs to be audacious.** You don't just work and hope and then work some more. You plan to win. It's not about stumbling into success or getting lucky. Most of us live "defensively," working hard enough to pay the bills and go on vacation for a week every year. We take jobs that limit our risk of dying, but also crush our chances of really living. Think big. Change the world.

3 **Plan to execute outside of the spotlight.** You can't plan to win if you are busy trying to get noticed. This is a hard lesson to learn, but a key one, if you are going to achieve outrageous success. Looking impressive and being impressive are quite different. Keeping up the façade of looking successful will steal years of honest destiny from you. It's a huge distraction. Just be amazing. People will notice. I promise.

4 **Plan to lose a time or two before you win.** That's how it happens most of the time. If you get it right the first time, you have to question how audacious your goal really was. You have to expect that you will probably get it completely wrong the first few (dozen) times you try. Recognize the valuable lessons of failure and plan to get back up and keep doing until you win.

83

GIVING MINDSET

If you want outrageous success,
you have to be extreme and you have to be disciplined.

But there is a huge problem with extreme behavior and
disciplined activity.

By *themselves*, they are inherently selfish endeavors.

Without something to offset them, you become obsessed
with *you*.

When what you do most of the time is about you, then you're probably not doing much that is worthwhile.

I know from personal experience how dangerous that can be. Selfish behavior can cost you everything you truly care about.

The offsetting balance to extreme behavior and disciplined activity is a giving mindset.

It's really that simple.

So let's talk about this for a minute.

Being a giving person sounds like a topic for Sunday Mass or a United Way advertising campaign. So any discussion about giving is usually shrugged off with a cavalier "we must be in church" aloofness.

And if you are focused on "success," it seems all wrong. Isn't giving in direct conflict with achieving success?

Frankly, giving doesn't even seem to go along with extreme behavior and disciplined activity.

After all, how does it make sense to fight for your dreams and then give it all away? We chuckle at the naïveté of such thinking.

It doesn't take too much thought to quickly run the numbers:

Every dollar you give away is less money in your pocket.

Every hour you give to help someone is less time to work toward your goals.

Every emotional investment depletes your armory.

At first glance, the idea of giving as a success strategy seems insanely counterintuitive.

But stay with me for a few minutes. Let's explore this.

We think that giving will take more from us than we are prepared to invest. We think that focusing on others first means that our dreams and goals might go unfulfilled.

Nothing could be more wrong.

I realize the idea that giving leads to success sounds radical, even unbelievable.

But open your mind to the possibilities. Open your mind to the truth:

Giving is one of the most consistently reliable strategies for long-term success.

You can't reap the benefits of extreme behavior and disciplined activity unless you also give.

The best high-performers are all-around good people. They are kind and classy.

Being a jerk doesn't magically make someone more successful.

Hollywood and generations of bad stereotypes have made us think that being a horrible person somehow super-qualifies us to be a superstar. It's simply not true.

In fact, selfish behavior is the single biggest obstacle to truly achieving extraordinary success in life.

The problem is not process or plans or people. The problem is our selfish intentions.

It's easy to become selfish – selfish in our goals, in our actions, in our thinking and about our future.

We only do "me" things. We only help if we think there's something in it for us. We only care if we are guilted or shamed into it.

And it's destroying us from the inside out.

Let's get EDGY about this, fast.

Selfish behavior will steal every dream you have. You'll make bad decisions, hurt good people and destroy any chance you have of making a lasting difference in the world.

Selfish behavior is probably affecting your career too. You're too busy "doing your thing" to be the outrageously successful person you really could be. If you're struggling to land deals, grow revenue or get a promotion, you might want to look at your behavior.

Do people seem to be avoiding you or enjoying your misery? Have they stopped backing you? Is no one around to support you when the chips are down and you really need some help?

Those are indicators of bad behavior, of bad, selfish behavior.

You can call it bad karma or bad mojo or whatever.

Or you can call it what it is – the results of your selfish behavior.

Selfish behavior limits your potential for greatness.

So maybe you change all that...starting today.

Giving requires an attitude shift. It starts with a mindset of focusing on others rather than yourself.

It's not just about what you do. It's how you see the world around you.

It doesn't mean that you don't work harder than you ever dreamed possible to achieve your goals. It means that you are tuned in to what's going on around you while you do it.

It means that you see your effort and your discipline – and your success – in the context of something bigger.

The fact remains that if you live a life that is all about you, then you miss out on the beauty of life coming together around you.

Maybe the solution is:

Giving instead of leveraging.

Helping instead of maneuvering.

Caring instead of manipulating.

Investing instead of executing.

Just be a good person. Care about others. Share your experience and talents. Contribute to the greater good.

You might not emerge as an ice-cold titan of industry. You might not even qualify for your company's "chairman's club."

But you'll find yourself strangely fulfilled, exceeding expectations and wildly in control of an amazing destiny.

Just ask Wayne Elsey.

Wayne sat on the edge of his couch on December 26, 2004. watching breaking news of a massive tsunami that had crashed into Indonesia, devastating millions of people's lives. The tsunami destroyed thousands of square miles of land, ripped buildings off their foundations and decimated town after town in a torrent of debris, twisted metal and anything else the raging water swept up in its path.

But it was when Wayne saw footage of a single shoe drifting slowly along a shoreline that the sheer vastness of this human tragedy hit home. It made him sick to his stomach.

As he sat there transfixed by the events happening halfway around the world, Wayne knew that this time he had to do more than "cut a check." He needed to get involved, to figure out a way to truly make a difference. He later said, "Before the 2004 Asian tsunami, I wasn't directly involved with any charities on a regular basis. I considered monetary donations to be sufficient, and I concentrated 100% on 'making the deal' happen in the for-profit world. That was my life before it changed dramatically. [After the tsunami] I was determined not to stand around with my hands in my pockets."

And so he started by doing what he had done most of his life – moving shoes. Wayne began stocking shelves for a local shoe company in Northern Virginia when he was just 15. By the time he graduated from high school, he was working for the company full time. At age 22, Wayne became the youngest vice president at Stride Rite, and by 23, he was regional vice president of a national chain of shoe stores. Just a few years later, he became CEO of a new shoe venture and proceeded to grow the business 400%.

Wayne Elsey knew the business of shoes. But this time he wasn't going to sell them. He was going to donate them.

He went to work with a passion, calling dozens of executives he had established relationships with over the years. He shared his idea and asked for help. In short order, Wayne had more than 250,000 pairs of new shoes to send to Indonesia. People who had lost everything would have something of their own – not just a pair of shoes, but hope. And what a difference hope made.

A year later, Hurricane Katrina ravaged the Gulf Coast of the United States. Wayne got back on the phone, asking the same people to do something bigger, to give more. This time, Wayne sent almost one million pairs of shoes to people in need.

That was when Wayne realized that he could make a bigger difference with his life by giving to others full time. So he started Soles4Souls, a nonprofit that puts shoes on feet and hope in hearts all over the world. Almost eight years later, with Wayne as CEO, Soles4Souls is one of the fastest-growing nonprofits in the country and has given 12 million pairs of shoes to needy people in 130 different countries.

But Wayne will tell you that he's just getting started. Rather than closing his next big shoe deal, today Wayne's goal is "to change people's lives with the gift of shoes."

A giving mindset can alter the trajectory of your life.

If you want to grow, you have to give...as a person, as a leader, in your career, in your business.

You'll never lose by giving more.

WHAT IS – AND IS NOT – **GIVING**

What makes this discussion about giving so challenging is our confusion around what giving really is.

Is it charity? Is it investment? Is it catharsis?

Maybe our confusion about the subject lies in how complex we've made it. And the fact that we sometimes confuse the verb "giving" for the actual thing.

We spend so much energy trying to pretend that we are givers that we've lost the essence of what giving really is.

Are you truly giving?

Or are you just going through the motions?

Consider this:

In Center, ND, a small town with fewer than 300 people, Hazel and Emmet and Myrdith lived in a small, simple home with their parents, William and Blanche. Fifteen-year-old Hazel was the oldest of the children and responsible enough to drive the horse and buggy to the one-room country school two miles away.

In the late morning of March 15, 1920, a blizzard began to move into the area. Concerned for the safety of the students, the teacher quickly dismissed them so they would have enough time to make it home safely. But Hazel's father was already on the way to get them in a sled pulled by the family's workhorse.

William reached the school before the children left and quickly settled them under the warm blankets in the sled. Telling them to wait for him, he went to the school barn to harness up the horse and buggy his children had brought in that morning. When he got back, the children and the sled were gone.

The driving wind and threatening storm clouds had spooked the old horse, and she had impatiently headed down the road toward home with the children. Soon the blizzard made it impossible for the horse or Hazel to see the road. The emptiness of the wide-open prairie and the blinding snow created complete confusion. Minutes turned into hours as the horse pulled the sled blindly through the blizzard. They were lost.

But that wasn't the worst of it. The sled hit an obstacle, sending it airborne. When it came down, it landed sideways, throwing the children into the slushy snow. Despite all their efforts, Hazel and her brother and sister couldn't push the sled upright.

Using the sled as a shelter against the driving wind, Hazel took the blankets and laid several of them on the snow. Telling Emmet and Myrdith to lie down, she gathered the remaining blankets and covered all three of them. And there they waited for their father to find them.

As they huddled in the snow, Hazel began to tell the younger children stories to keep their minds occupied. They sang songs they had learned in school. They recited Scripture and other essays they had memorized. And when they got sleepy, Hazel would pinch them and remind them that they mustn't fall asleep.

At some point, the wind changed directions, and the blankets kept blowing away, exposing the children. Telling her siblings to move together, Hazel wrapped the top blankets tightly over and around Emmet and Myrdith and then lay down on top of them, using her body weight to keep the blankets secured.

As the driving snow began to build up around the huddled children, Hazel kicked it away with her feet. Each time, she moved a little more slowly. And then, with an almost inaudible groan, she stopped moving completely.

More than 20 hours after the children left the school yard, a search team found tracks in the snow that led them to the upturned sled, still harnessed to Old Maude standing patiently in the snow. As the rescuers brushed off the last, thin layer of snow covering the sled, they gasped at what they saw: Hazel, unmoving, lying with her arms outstretched over the blanketed Emmet and Myrdith. In a final gesture of unselfish love, she had unbuttoned her coat and used it to cover her brother and sister, who were still alive.

At Hazel's funeral, the minister summed up Hazel's selfless gift with a reading from the Bible: "Greater love hath no man than when he lays down his life for his friend."

Hazel became an American hero in her passing. Called "the Guardian Angel of the Prairies," she and her story drew national attention. Hospitals, orphanages, even Ford Motor Company, used her memory as an inspiring call to action – a reminder that what really moves us to acts of greatness is selflessness.

Today, outside the Oliver County Courthouse in North Dakota stands a monument inscribed with the following words: "In memory of Hazel Miner. To the dead a tribute, to the living a memory, to posterity an inspiration."

When you give, you change people's lives.

It's that simple.

And there is no other way you can get that result.

––––––––––––––––

So what is giving, and how do we do it right?

Sometimes it's helpful to break down an emotional topic like giving. Let's talk about what giving is – and what it's not.

GIVING IS A GIFT.

Giving is not trading.

Trading is exchanging one thing for another. And there is nothing wrong with trading. It's the oldest form of successful business.

But don't confuse the two activities.

Giving and trading lead to different results.

Giving means that you "gift" something – no strings attached.

You can't trade your way to making a difference. You have to give your way there.

GIVING EXPECTS NOTHING IN RETURN.

Giving doesn't have a planned "return on investment." By definition, it's an investment *without* an expected return.

You only set yourself up for disappointment when you pretend to give, expecting the recipient to give you something back.

That's not how giving works.

It's better to not give at all than to go through the motions with mental strings attached.

If you give in order to feel better about yourself...

If you give to avoid or appease your guilt...

If you give because you want attention or notoriety...

Then it's not giving at all.

Giving is about you focusing on the other person.

It's not about you. Or another notch on your belt.

Frankly, it can't be about you. If it were about you, it would be called "getting." Which isn't even close to the idea of giving.

When you give expecting nothing in return, you change people's lives.

It's not an act. It's a result.

GIVING COSTS YOU SOMETHING.

It's not giving if there is no value to what is given. Just because I give you something doesn't mean it's a gift.

You can't just dump your leftovers on someone and expect them to be grateful.

That is called throwing things away, right? And no one feels good being on the receiving end of a sham "give-a-thon."

It's easy to pretend that what you are offering is valuable when it's not.

Giving has to cost you. It does. And the more you want to give, the more it's going to cost you.

To start giving, take something that really means something to you – time, money, attention, energy, emotions – and give it away.

It was almost 100 years ago that Hazel Miner gave her life for her brother and sister. Her gift inspired a country.

The same principle of giving stands the test of time.

Her story forces us to pause and think about who we are and what we are living for. It makes us question if we really are giving or just going through the motions.

Did Hazel Miner know when she lay down on top of her siblings to protect them that she would give the ultimate gift?

We'll never know. But we do know one thing for sure.

It wasn't a trade. It wasn't a "take turns" proposition with her brother and sister. She gave, expecting nothing in return.

She gave something incredibly precious and valuable and meaningful. And that gift made a real difference.

I'm not suggesting that you give your life for another.

I'm suggesting that you give OF your life to others.

I'm suggesting that you might not be giving enough.

When you are gone, will anyone build a monument to you?

Will the efforts of your life stand the test of time?

Perhaps it's time to change how you think about giving.

Perhaps there is a big lesson to be learned from a young girl who gave what she had.

GIVING **STARTS WITH GRATITUDE**

Giving is rooted in gratitude.

We struggle with giving because we don't take the time to think about how much we really have.

If we are convinced we have nothing, we have nothing to give away.

Sometimes it takes startling reminders to help us appreciate how much we have to give – moments in life when just how much we have to be thankful for is thrust upon us.

Not too long ago, I was working with a client located about an hour north of Philadelphia, PA. After a long day of strategy, I was exhausted and stressed out and not in the most positive state of mind. So I decided to do what I do to relax – lace up the running shoes and go for a run.

The town was in a valley surrounded by mountains, so I set out with GPS in hand and headed for a nearby peak, running up steep mountain trails. When I reached the top, it was about 7:30, and the sun was just beginning to set. A ball of orange fire at the edge of the horizon. So beautiful.

As I sat alone watching a breathtaking sunset, my attitude began to mellow. How could I be stressed out seeing such a spectacular sight? Truly, life was great. The world was amazing, and I was seeing it with my eyes, feeling it deep in my soul.

After a while, I realized that it was getting dark and that I was a dozen miles from my hotel. So I put in my ear buds, turned on my music and started back. But instead of heading back down the same way I had come up, I took a road down the back of the mountain, hoping it would be a faster route "home."

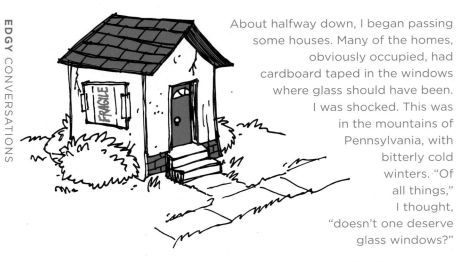

About halfway down, I began passing some houses. Many of the homes, obviously occupied, had cardboard taped in the windows where glass should have been. I was shocked. This was in the mountains of Pennsylvania, with bitterly cold winters. "Of all things," I thought, "doesn't one deserve glass windows?"

As I ran, I contemplated the sadness of what I was seeing. And I was suddenly profoundly grateful for the fact that I have glass windows in my house. Yes, it's a small thing to me – something that before that day I had never even thought about. But it is probably a pretty big deal to the people living in those houses in the dead of winter.

I arrived back at my hotel full of gratitude, moved by what I'd seen – the beauty of the sunset and the despair of poverty. And I was changed.

The truth is, few of us are truly grateful for what we have.

Gratitude is a powerful attitude changer.

And it is the foundation of a giving mindset.

That experience changed my perspective about a lot of things.

It changed my perspective about what I have to give.

Perhaps you're thinking, "Dan, you seem to be a successful guy. Of course you have plenty to be grateful for. It's easy to be grateful when you have a great life."

True.

But that's a lame excuse.

Anyone can have gratitude and be a truly giving person.

Clay Dyer proves that.

As far back as he can remember, there was nothing Clay wanted to do more than become a professional fisherman. From the time he was five years old, he spent hours each day with a rod and reel practicing the perfect cast. Fishing was Clay's world. After school. On the weekends. Anytime he could get away, he was on the water trying to catch something.

And his practice paid off. He could cast with pinpoint accuracy – overhand, sidearm, even flip-and-pitch. Those who knew Clay best bragged that he could cast a quarter-ounce metal fishing lure into a cup from 50 feet away. His skills were impressive.

At the age of 15, Clay began entering professional fishing tournaments. He quickly became known for his fiercely competitive nature. Over the next nine years, he fished in more than 200 bass tournaments. He won 25 of those events and came close to winning several dozen more, which is a staggering win percentage – especially considering Clay's circumstances.

Clay Dyer was born on a Tuesday in late May 1978. The doctors weren't sure if he would live. He was born without any legs, no left arm and only a partial arm attached to his right shoulder. But he did live.

While others considered him severely handicapped, Clay thought he had a pretty good life. "I knew I had a heart, a soul and a mind, which is what really makes a human being," Clay has shared. "Anything else you have is a bonus."

That attitude has enabled Clay to be a high performer. And fishing wasn't the only competitive sport that he tried to master. Growing up, Clay played baseball with his neighborhood friends. All the way up through junior high school, he played first base and swung a bat. (He used a designated runner to run the bases for him.)

As a professional bass fisherman, his physical limitations, while daunting, pose less of a challenge. Even though he weighs just under 90 pounds and is about 40 inches tall, he can drive a boat, cast a pinpoint fishing line, bait a hook and tie knots with his teeth, and wrangle a fighting bass into the boat...and be a winner doing it.

Clay's motto for life is, "If I can, you can."

"God wanted me to be successful at fishing," he tells audiences who come to hear him speak. "I'm glad I was made this way. I was born to be a superstar."

Sure, Clay has a relentless determination to compete. And he put in the outrageous amounts of effort and discipline it took to be a superstar.

But gratitude enables him to maximize his capabilities. Instead of sulking and complaining, he is thankful for what he can do and the opportunities he has.

And gratitude enables him to give more.

Clay spends the majority of his time sharing his life experiences with charities, churches and organizations. He is also a volunteer athletic coach at a high school.

Gratitude and a giving mindset allow him to be incredibly successful.

The same exact principles apply to you and your situation.

If you're like many people, gratitude doesn't come naturally. It requires practice and effort.

And it isn't something you practice once a year while holding hands with family members around a carved turkey.

Gratitude is a habit you can develop.

So how about if you work on that?

How about if you start complaining less and giving more?

BE EDGY
PRACTICE GRATITUDE

1 Look for the good in every situation. It's hard to be thankful when all you see is misery and sadness. Force yourself to look for the happy moments in life – for what is good and noble and inspiring. Your brain will kick into grateful mode and start noticing all the good things going on around you. What you set out to find, you will usually discover. Imagine how easy it is to be grateful when everything around you is good.

2 Write it all down; read it all back. There is something very powerful about putting awesome things on paper. It kind of makes the experience official. And what better way to stay motivated than to reread previous triumphs? By writing down all the positive things in your life, you create a buffer between your fears and reality. It's all there on paper, in black and white.

3 Stop running around; slow it down. The busyness of life has most of us so worried and frantic that we rarely pause long enough to see things as they really are...to see how good we really have it. You need to start stopping. Whether you meditate, exercise or just take time alone to read a book, slow down and let the beauty of life emerge.

4 Say "thank you" more often. Exercising gratitude is a powerful igniter of creativity. Saying "thank you" is mental, in a good way. Just saying the words puts you in a better mood. Teach yourself to say the words and then use them often. They are a "gateway drug" to the real thing.

5 Laugh at yourself. Taking life too seriously is a big reason why we aren't more grateful. Sometimes just laughing at our circumstances is the breakthrough perspective that enables us to find a new way to be successful. You can be aggressive all you want, but seeing the absurdity of what happens to you is a powerful way to put yourself in a position to take advantage of each opportunity.

GIVING **IS** TRANSFORMATIONAL

There's no easy way around this subject. So let's jump in with the understanding that this discussion might be uncomfortable for you.

For the most part, we are pretty good at giving...especially when it's convenient or socially popular.

We give when it's easy to give.

And that's not blaming or pointing the finger at anyone.

That's just how we're wired.

Our brains are essentially risk/reward calculators. We assess each giving opportunity (usually without consciously thinking about it) and decide how to behave based on how big the "reward" is.

And we each assess giving differently. How we look at giving depends on how we normally view anything else in our lives.

Those who are especially intellectual give when the occasion merits or when they can logically justify that giving is a better decision than not giving.

Those who make decisions from a more emotional framework give when they feel that it's the best course of action. They give to show that they care or because they like to see the joy of appreciation.

Neither is right nor wrong. Just different.

Regardless of *how* you make the decision, the point is that you decide when, what and how to give.

Now, you probably believe that you are a giving person. You can probably recite a half-dozen examples of how you are different, how you really are a giver.

But I challenge you to rethink that.

You see, most of the giving you say that you do isn't really giving at all.

It's simply activity.

You write a check. You volunteer at an event. You go to a meeting. You have dinner with your spouse. You show up for the recital or the game.

And you think you are engaged.

But if you are constantly texting or checking email or thinking about something else, are you really engaged and involved?

You're there, but you're not. Present in body but not in mind or spirit. Just doing your obligatory time.

But the essence of giving is doing it when it's hard and inconvenient. When volunteering doesn't fit your schedule. When you have to love somebody who might not deserve it at the time. When you've been hurt, and you want to focus on yourself first.

Think about it for a moment. Are you truly giving? Or are you going through the motions, checking off the giving "boxes"?

It's okay to admit it. We all do it. We all pretend to give.

But people know the difference.

People know when you really care and when you are putting a friendly smile on your selfish behavior.

The motions of pretend giving and real giving are the same. Just like the motions of riding a stationary bike and a street bike are the same. In both cases, your legs are pumping, and you're sweating like crazy. But on the stationary bike, you're not going anywhere.

Pretend giving and authentic giving may look the same on the surface and may involve the same actions. But they are vastly different.

The difference is a personal and emotional investment.

Giving requires you to be vulnerable. It means you might get hurt. And that's probably not something you're comfortable with. Who wants more pain in their lives?

So you stop truly giving and replace it with a bunch of other activities that you pretend are the same thing.

You walk out the door or end the call with, "*I love you.*" But you won't stop to give your loved ones your full, undivided attention when they need to talk to you.

You spend "quality time" with your kids while you watch TV, surf the Internet on your tablet or obsess about problems at work.

You go through the steps of giving all the time without ever really connecting emotionally.

You have fooled yourself into believing that what you're doing is giving. *It's not.*

It's not enough to be present in body only.

It's not enough to write a check and expect someone else to do the work. Don't get me wrong – giving money is undeniably helpful and important. But sometimes it isn't enough.

You have to get involved. You have to give part of your life, your time, your heart, your emotions.

The most powerful forms of giving have nothing to do with money at all. They have to do with the deeply personal and emotional aspects of human nature – belief, moral support, connection, kindness.

Giving is easy when all you have to do is pull out your checkbook and sign your name.

Giving gets a little stickier when you have to invest emotion and time into someone or something else. Giving is much harder to do emotionally than financially.

When giving is simply an activity or a series of activities, it is transactional.

Giving becomes transformational when you invest yourself in the effort.

But that personal investment is what giving is all about.

It's about putting yourself out there emotionally. Giving and loving when you can't force the other person to give to you or love you back.

It's why giving is so difficult.

And so transformational.

Michael was at the end of his rope. A retired paramedic, he was now homeless – living out of his van, moving from city to city, making money from the few odd jobs he was able to hustle.

That's when he met her.

He was walking down a busy street one day when he saw a woman having a seizure. Convulsing, she fell to the ground. Busy morning commuters simply walked around her, most not even bothering to look as she lay there moaning. But Michael sprang into action. Pushing through the crowd, he cleared a space around the woman and began CPR. He told a passerby to call 911. Eventually, he was able to stabilize the woman and stayed with her, holding her hand, until the ambulance arrived.

He had no money, no home, not even enough gas in his beat-up van to drive the woman to the hospital. But Michael gave what he had – himself.

When the woman – we'll call her "Ann" – got out of the hospital, she asked Michael to spend an afternoon with her and her family. That's when she found out he was homeless. His gift of kindness seemed all the more special given his own problems at the time.

Wanting to give back to the person who had given so much to her, Ann rented Michael a hotel room for the week. And when the week was over, he packed up his van and set out to find another day job. Before he left, she asked for his disposable cell phone number so that they might stay in touch. Michael wasn't even sure he would have enough money to keep the number live, but he shared it anyway, never expecting to hear from her again.

But it wasn't long before Ann called to check on him. And that call led to more calls. And the calls turned into a friendship – a friendship between a man who gave what he had and a woman who needed that gift. And the woman gave, too. She gave friendship to a man who was alone in the world.

A few months later when Ann got sick again, Michael didn't stop to think twice. He begged and borrowed the 250-miles-worth of gas money he needed to get to her. That was the last time they were apart. Michael married Ann, and together they opened a successful painting company.

Michael's gift transformed his life. He met his soul mate and found love. He discovered the courage to get back on his feet, to find happiness and success and inspiration. Now he uses that gift to transform other people's lives.

Each Christmas, Michael and Ann find three or four homeless, out-of-luck people and pay for them to stay in a hotel through the holidays. Each night, they bring these people home-cooked meals and warm clothing, and help them reconnect with lost family and friends.

Several of these people whom Michael and Ann have helped are now off the streets, working jobs and back in touch with their families. One has even followed Michael's example and helps several more homeless people every year around Christmastime.

Michael's giving was transformational – for himself and for others. His gift changed the world in ways he never could have imagined. And it all started with just one act of selfless giving from a man who had nothing to give.

You too can change the world in ways you cannot possibly imagine.

You just have to stop pretending and start giving.

Give from your heart not your head.

When you invest *yourself*, giving moves from transactional to transformational, from something you do to who you are.

I've said that giving shouldn't be about you and that you shouldn't give with the expectation of receiving. And that is all true.

But it is also true that you do benefit when you genuinely give of yourself from the heart.

You do get something in exchange.

You become a better you.

Y(H)UMAN
STRATEGY

In 1960, Cassius Clay won the light heavyweight gold
medal for boxing in the Rome Summer Olympics after
competing in more than 100 amateur fights and losing less
than a handful. An athlete with massive talent, he physically
dominated his opponents in the ring.

Yet back in the United States just a few weeks later, he was
thrown out of a "whites only" diner in Louisville, KY.
Disgusted by the bigotry of the countrymen he had
represented, he threw his Olympic gold medal in the Ohio
River. The ability to overcome being treated unfairly would
later help him become a world champion.

Five years later, Cassius Clay, now known as Muhammad Ali, took on Sonny Liston in a fight Ali entered as a 7-to-1 underdog. Through the first three rounds, Ali was clearly winning on points. Fast and powerful, he had already bruised Liston and cut him below both eyes. Ali was about to pull off the upset of the year.

But Liston, fearing he would lose the fight and the championship, smeared a substance on his gloves hoping to temporarily blind Ali so that he could end the fight with a knockout blow and avoid embarrassment.

Unable to see, his eyes stinging deeply, Ali danced outside Liston's reach until his sweat and tears washed away enough of the poison so he could fight. And that's what he did – second by second, minute by minute – until the round was over. Despite being treated unfairly yet again, Ali knew that if he could make it through the next round, he had the fight won. He knew that Liston had resorted to cheating because he was running scared.

Ali entered the ring in the next round with the focus to dominate his opponent and gave Liston a beating. Broken physically and mentally, Liston was unable to answer the bell for the start of round seven and conceded the battle to Ali.

Muhammad Ali was unquestionably a great fighter, but not because he had the best skills or was born with incredible talent. In fact, he went on to lose championships to Joe Frazier, Leon Spinks and Larry Holmes. (He later won back the championships from Frazier and Spinks.)

But Ali was a phenomenal exhibitionist. That's what made him extraordinarily successful. He was amazingly skilled at working the press, the public and the crowd. People had never seen a boxer with such charisma. He used his words to both entertain and provoke people. And he understood perhaps better than any other boxer how to get inside his opponents' heads – how to dominate them not just physically but mentally.

More than 30 years after his last fight, Muhammad Ali is arguably still the best known and one of the most beloved and revered athletes in the world. In the end, his phenomenal success was driven as much by his understanding of human nature as his physical prowess.

Just because you are talented doesn't necessarily mean you will be successful in life.

Even if you're putting in the effort.

Even with an extreme dedication to learning, you can't "out smart" your way to being amazing.

Brains and brawn aren't enough.

Neither is a mind-blowing amount of discipline, although it contributes wildly to consistently successful outcomes.

Not effort. Not extreme behavior. Not discipline. Not even giving.

All of these are still not enough.

Muhammad Ali's story shows us that achieving outrageous success takes something more.

It takes a human strategy.

It takes insight into how people think. It takes understanding how pain and fear drive people's actions. And it takes knowing how to emotionally connect with people.

Having a human strategy is the key differentiator between those who achieve outrageous success and those who don't.

The truth is that much of your success in life hinges on your ability to understand people.

Without that nuance, you are like a robot – great at handling the logical, black-and-white issues of life when 2+2=4.

But life is rarely black and white. It's a million shades of gray.

Most people think that logic drives human behavior. But that's not how it happens.

It is emotion that drives behavior. Irrational, illogical emotion.

And that awareness is vital to your ability to achieve the results you want.

Every decision you make in life is impacted by how well you understand people, their behavior and the way they think.

Having a great marriage, enjoying good relationships, landing a job, being promoted, commanding the compensation you think you deserve. It's all linked to the way you deal with the people around you.

So many people fail because they don't understand that things are always different than what they appear to be. Situations and circumstances are usually not what they seem to be. People typically don't mean what they say.

Which is why you have to have a strategy for navigating the human element of life – which, frankly, is almost all of it.

It's an awareness that does not expect rational behavior and instead anticipates the illogic of deeply personal life experiences.

Some call it having good people skills or emotional intelligence. Regardless of the terminology, you need a strategy for connecting and communicating with other people.

And before you shrug off the idea of a human strategy as the whimsical weakness of "couch-potato lifers," you might want to take a closer look.

Emotional intelligence is what enabled Steve Jobs to create a passionate following for Apple's technology. He believed that the user experience is more important than functionality.

He was right.

And that idea resonated profoundly with consumers who were enamored by technology that looked good and worked effortlessly. That emotional connection between company and customer fueled a 9,000% increase in Apple's market value during a period in which Microsoft increased in value only 5% and Intel rose only 14%.

It was emotion over logic; understanding people over pushing product.

The same knowledge that created one of the most valuable companies in the world can empower you as well.

Because you can't be an emotional nitwit and expect to produce the results you think you deserve.

You have to look beneath the surface and see others as human beings. You have to understand:

1	2	3
How pain and fear drive human behavior.	How the human brain makes decisions.	How love makes all the difference.

Without these insights, you will fail to motivate others to follow you. You won't have the ability to identify and fix the core issues that are negatively impacting your performance.

Without a people strategy, it's all too easy to exploit and manipulate people in your quest for success. A lack of emotional intelligence drives people away and alienates those who could help you achieve your goals.

And there is one more thing you need to understand: *Why*. Why any of this even matters.

The purpose of a human strategy is not to manipulate others. It's to connect with people and help them to become better.

To make yourself better.

You see, the first step in a human strategy is to fix *the human within*. To fix *you*.

This matters because *you* matter. Figuring out *you* is important.

It starts with understanding your humanity. It's the relentless pursuit of learning about *you*, solving *you,* healing *you*.

Before you play doctor on those around you, you have to be able to cure yourself. Or at least understand what the cure is. You can't help other people until you can be completely honest about your own hang-ups and screw-ups.

A human strategy applies to *you* first.

Consider this...

Maybe your problems aren't *them* (everyone around you). Maybe everyone around you *isn't* an idiot. Maybe your emotions are making *you* one.

You might be the idiot you think other people are.

And that's okay. You're human. You are limited by the realities of being human and the unpredictabilities of the other humans you live and work and play with.

Seek first to accept your own frailties. To fix the quirks in your own humanity.

Then you can work on the quirks in the humanity around you.

To do that, you need a strategy that is honest and kind, patient and relentless.

And completely human.

HOW PAIN AND FEAR **DRIVE YOUR ACTIONS**

You were born a winner.

And life taught you how to be a loser.

Ironic, isn't it?

You beat the odds. From conception, through nine months of prenatal nurturing, to emergence into a world full of dangers, you survived.

You were born fearless, however small and frail. You didn't know what you could or could not do. So you tried everything:

You explored the boundaries of sight, sound, touch, taste and smell.

You screamed until you could talk. And then you wouldn't stop talking.

You pulled the tablecloth off the table so you could see what was on top.

You licked anything in sight, from the bathroom floor to the dirty window. Germs didn't bother you.

You reached out to touch the hot stove even after your mother yelled at you 17 times that it would burn you.

You were curious about everything, from roly-poly bugs to why the sky is blue.

You believed you could do anything, go anywhere, be whatever you wanted to be when you grew up.

And then, you learned that you weren't supposed to do those things. You were told that you needed to "grow up and stop dreaming," to be "reasonable" and to not set your expectations too high.

Any of that sound familiar?

You've had these limitations drummed into you for years.

It's all wonderfully defensible "just trying to keep your feet on the ground" nonsense, guaranteed to neuter your ambition, bankrupt your dreams and keep you thoroughly despondent.

I understand that your parents and teachers and peers had good intentions and didn't want you to get hurt. But in telling you "no," they crushed your spirit of adventure and imagination.

And they taught you to be afraid of anything that might cause you pain.

So you stopped taking chances. Stopped putting yourself out there so you wouldn't get hurt.

You learned to live small, believing that you were unable to be amazing.

Over time, whether you realized it or not, pain and fear started turning you into a loser. And you've been fighting to get back into the winner's circle ever since.

Pain and fear are two of the greatest influencers of human behavior.

Pain happens...and fear reminds you of it later.

Pain is what hurts you. Fear is what never lets you forget about it.

Pain and fear are holding you back. Undoing every dream. Destroying the advantages you gain through your effort and discipline and giving.

And they will crush your spirit and devour your soul if you let them.

But it doesn't have to be that way.

So let's talk about it.

Pain is the primary driver of everything you do. (Or don't do, for that matter.)

Every effort, every strategy, every tactic is focused on avoiding pain.

Pain determines what you think about and what you believe is possible.

The problem with pain is that much of the time, it isn't physical.

The experience and expression of pain changes over time.

You stop scraping your knees, getting bloody noses and breaking bones.

You move from the playgrounds of childhood to the battlegrounds of life, from the swing set to the headset.

Now, you scar your heart and your mind instead of your knees.

It's mental ache, not muscle ache.

Betrayal. Loss. Abandonment. Failure. The standard things that life throws at all of us.

And that kind of pain runs deep. Very deep.

Emotional pain is gripping and intense. And it doesn't go

away quickly. Sometimes it never does.

You know what I'm talking about. It's the gritty side of life that you desperately try to forget. It's the personal pain that chokes the life out of your dreams and ambitions.

It's trauma in every imaginable sense of the word. So much so that you will do just about anything to avoid going through that experience of emotional pain and stress again.

Over time, you become less and less willing to engage in activities that might lead to pain. Eventually, avoiding pain becomes a subconscious activity.

And while it may seem like you are eliminating pain from your life, nothing could be further from the truth.

You just get better at hiding it from others.

And from yourself.

You don't talk about what scares you the most.

You become an expert at pretending that everything is all right. And you might even be able to convince yourself if it weren't for the shadows on the wall.

Just about the time you think you're whole again, you see the shadows cast by past painful experiences. And you start to relive them.

In reality, there is nothing there. But you are affected by the pain you think you see.

And you're frightened, because you've been taught to fear pain. Your breath comes a little faster and your heart starts to beat a little quicker. All of your senses tell you that you are about to get hurt.

That fear drives you to run away. To run away from something that isn't there.

The shadows on the wall are stealing your destiny.

But what if your eyes are deceiving you?

What if the shadow of past pain is nothing more than a

mechanical pencil wedged between a pizza box and the edge of the couch?

What if the shadows don't tell the right story about your past? Or they tell just one story of pain when there are many stories of success and happiness?

Maybe it's nothing more than your mind playing tricks on you.

Maybe the harder you look, the closer you look, the less you find to fear.

Maybe you turn on the light of truth and the shadows disappear in an instant.

We all have pain. We all see shadows.

Each of us has a choice: to live in the shadows or to turn on the lights.

And it is a choice.

———

Fear is the beginning of mediocrity.

It keeps you from being a high performer. It makes you feel irrationally inadequate, compels you to think you might not be good enough.

It's fear that says to you, "You can't take a new job," even though your current job is crappy. "You have a mortgage; you have kids. What are you thinking?"

It's fear that replies, "I'm afraid I don't know" when you're asked a question you might not have the answer to.

It's fear that concedes, "I'm afraid you're right" when the facts suggest a point of view different than your own.

It's fear that responds, "I'm afraid to ask" when you hear that bad news awaits you.

You think your fear is protecting you. But it's making you a person who can't act, who won't take risks.

And when you fear to act, you can't achieve outrageously amazing things.

Once upon a time, winning was all you knew how to do.

Sure, you took it one breath and one step at a time. But it worked...you won. And you won consistently.

You were all you needed to succeed.

The only thing that has changed is that the world has scared you into believing that you might not be enough, might not have enough, to be outrageously successful.

The same courage that made you a winner as a child gets all twisted up by the time you are old enough to read books like this one.

But you can return to that fearlessness you had as a child.

You have everything you need to be successful right now. You are capable of achieving every success you can ever imagine.

Do you fully understand that?

The only thing standing in the way of your success is you. Your biggest enemy is the person you see in the mirror.

But it's not your lack of education, your financial situation or the bad decisions you've made that are holding you back.

It is the fear of what you could achieve if you believed in yourself.

As Marianne Williamson so eloquently noted in her book, *A Return to Love:* "Our deepest fear is not that we are inadequate. Our deepest fear is that we are powerful beyond measure. It is our light, not our darkness, that most frightens us."

It's you being afraid of your full potential.

It's all just fear. And it's not real.

It's time to stop making excuses and become the winner you're afraid you really are.

Looking past pain and overcoming fear are the keys to outrageous acts of courage.

All the odds pointed to Derek Redmond being the winner of the 400-meter sprint at the 1992 Olympic Games in Barcelona. He had already won the World Championships, European Championships and the Commonwealth Games and was the British record holder.

Within the first 150 meters of the semi-final race, Derek surged to the front of the pack, running at a blistering pace that was sure to set a new Olympic record. Suddenly, without warning, he fell to the ground in excruciating pain. His hamstring muscle had completely torn away from the bone. Lying crumpled on the track, he thought about his dying dream of Olympic gold.

As the other runners crossed the finish line, medics hurried to Derek with a stretcher to help him off the track. It was in that moment that Derek created a story that the world will never forget.

He stood up.

In spite of the alarms screaming in his brain and without a muscle attaching his pelvis to his leg, he started to hobble the remaining 250 meters to the finish line. Swinging his arms madly, he jumped forward as best he could on his one good leg.

Step after agonizing step.

From the stadium, an older man fought his way through the crowd and the security guards trying to hold him back. Once on the track, he ran to his son, placed his arm under Derek's shoulder and began to walk slowly around the track with him.

"You don't have to do this," his father said.

"Yes, I do," was all Derek could say, the pain so intense that he winced between words and the disappointment so unbearable that tears streamed down his face.

And so with a father holding a son, and a son holding a leg that didn't have a muscle to move it, they headed toward the finish line. As 65,000 fans stood and watched, transfixed by the scene unfolding in front of them, Derek's father paused a few feet before the finish line so that Derek could finish on his own.

Two decades later, no one remembers who won that race. But millions of us remember the spirit of a man who refused to quit.

Derek Redmond should have quit.

Quitting wouldn't have just been easier. It would have been the right thing to do. It would have been the logical thing to do. It was what he was supposed to do.

So why didn't he quit?

Freakish determination? Maybe.

Or maybe he knew that the long-term emotional pain of not seeing his dream through to the end would have been far greater than the short-term physical pain he would have to suffer. Maybe he didn't want to live with the pain of regret for the rest of his life.

Or maybe he simply made the decision to finish what he started, despite the pain.

That's hard. It's difficult to even describe how hard that is.

I've been there before – facing all-consuming pain and fear.

Maybe you have, too.

It's so hard to keep going sometimes that you really can't conceive how to make it.

In that moment, you have to make the choice to be awesome, to be extraordinary.

You might have some cynical thoughts about the "Just Do It" flavor of those words, but the cynics are the people left behind complaining.

The people who have the courage to make the choice are the ones who matter.

Don't let pain and fear make you a loser.

Choose to look past the pain.

Choose to be more courageous. Fear drives you to run from pain. Courage helps you to heal it.

Those are the choices you make every time you decide not to quit.

And when you decide that despite the pain, the tears, the fear, the failure – despite all that – you will not quit, you will have broken through.

HOW YOUR BRAIN **MAKES** DECISIONS

Understanding how the human brain works is the foundation of a human strategy.

In fact, the whole concept falls apart pretty darn quickly if you don't know how the brain computes information.

On the other hand, you can accomplish just about anything if you understand how the brain makes decisions and its powerful effect on your performance.

Studies show that simply knowing how your brain works actually makes you smarter.

Just being aware causes you to be more thoughtful about your behaviors.

When you become aware of the pain and fear in your life, you can choose to react differently.

Awareness gives you a path through the pain and fear.

Awareness allows you to take control of any situation. And that is very empowering.

You think you know how your brain works, right? After all, you have one and you try to use it as often as possible.

Think again.

The human brain is a complex computer, ingesting millions of data points from your senses every few minutes and rendering instantaneous analysis and options based on your past experiences, beliefs, biases and education.

Yet despite all this complexity, the brain consistently defaults to a decision-making process based on a few primal instincts.

The human brain hasn't really changed all that much since the beginning of mankind. After hundreds of years of hypotheses on how the brain works, advanced technology like MRI scans reaffirms how very primitive it still is.

There are three main ways the brain handles any information it receives:

1	2	3
If it's boring or expected, the brain ignores it.	If it's too complex, the brain dramatically summarizes it.	If it's threatening, the brain prepares the body to fight or run.

Subconsciously, the brain reverts to one of these three defaults as it attempts to capture, catalog and understand what is going on around us. And inside us.

Everyone's brain is essentially wired the same way. But each of us views the world differently.

That unique perspective shapes how we interpret what happens around us and to us. And that interpretation drives our responses and our reactions.

Your interpretation of events and circumstances depends on your own life experiences, your view of the world. Without you giving it much thought, your subconscious mind tilts the world toward your biases, good and bad.

That's how you see things – not rationally or realistically, but how you experience them.

Never mind the fact that your view may be completely wrong.

Your brain processes pain and fear the same way.

You see a situation and interpret it as painful even though it might not be threatening at all. You may only be seeing shadows on the wall.

The most powerful brain response to pain and fear is "fight or flight." Even the smallest hint of an uncomfortable or threatening situation can push your entire nervous system into overdrive.

Within fractions of a second, the amygdala part of your brain sparks electrical impulses throughout your sympathetic nervous system to activate your adrenal glands. These glands dump adrenaline into your bloodstream. Instantly, that adrenaline increases your breathing, heart rate and blood pressure, and winds up your muscles to burst into action when needed. The blood vessels in your skin narrow to limit bleeding if you are wounded. Saliva stops flowing (so your mouth becomes dry), and your digestive system shuts down to conserve energy.

It all happens automatically. Often without you even being aware of it.

And this triggering happens all of the time. Your brain is constantly looking for opportunities to be fearful, for things that seem threatening.

And it's constantly expanding its database of things it finds frightening or emotionally traumatic. A job interview. An argument with your spouse. Someone criticizing you in a meeting. The possibility of failure, of not achieving your goals.

In today's world, there are no sabre tooth tigers trying to eat you alive. The threats are altogether different.

But they are just as frightening. And just as real.

At least in your mind.

In response to these perceived threats, you either become defensive and aggressive (fight) or disconnect and avoid the situation (flight).

And all that works great. Except for one thing.

Fear distorts your view of reality.

When fear grips you, it's temporary insanity. You react irrationally. Emotions start flying.

Of course, it seems rational to you because it's based on what you think you see and how you interpret the situation.

But looks can be deceiving. In fact, very little in life turns out to be exactly what you perceive it to be in your mind.

Here's a general rule of life:

It's always what it's not.

That's right. Appearances lie. What you interpret is different than reality. What you see is not what you get.

And that is why you react irrationally to the data your brain is capturing. (You do realize that the irrational behavior you find inexcusable in others comes from the same default wiring found in *your* brain, right?)

You become confused, unsure of what to do. You want to stop being anxious, fearful, uncertain. But you don't know how.

The answer is really quite simple: Take off the "fear goggles."

Disarm fear by seeking the truth.

Take control of your thinking.

Controlling your thoughts is the hardest part of struggling toward success. There is nothing more difficult. No bigger challenge.

And frankly, nothing more important.

Let's face it. The journey to success is brutal. You will get bruised and battered along the way.

Above all else, you have to be mentally tough.

Freddie Chapman understood all too well the importance of being mentally tough.

In 1930, 23-year-old Freddie Chapman led a British expedition to Greenland. He experienced such ferocious cold that he lost all of his fingernails and toenails. During one outing, he fell into a glacial crevasse and just barely saved himself by holding onto the handles of his dog sled and pulling himself, hand over hand, back to the top. On another outing, he got lost at sea and spent 20 hours in a kayak. He was one of only three people to survive the expedition.

Skip forward more than a decade.

British Army Capt. Frederick Chapman almost single-handedly thwarted the Japanese invasion of Malaysia during World War II. For four years, he led guerrilla warfare missions behind enemy lines.

In 1945, two years into his stay, he completely ran out of supplies, and everyone in his unit was lost to either gunfire or disease. For the next 100 weeks, he suffered from malaria and dysentery and endured skin-eating leeches. His boots wore out, and he walked barefoot through the jungle. He was captured by both Japanese forces and rogue Chinese bandits – and escaped from both. He succumbed to pneumonia, jungle fever and typhus and was unconscious for 17 days. He was wounded by a bomb and shot in the arm.

Yet Capt. Chapman survived, against all odds. Not only did he survive, he was outrageously "successful." He was responsible for destroying 7 supply trains, 15 bridges, 40 tanks and armored vehicles, and hundreds of Japanese troops. One man. All by himself.

Talk about being mentally tough.

Was Chapman afraid throughout his ordeal during the war? Unquestionably! Probably every single day. Wouldn't you be?

But his training in Greenland years earlier gave him the mindset he needed to survive. From his expedition experience, he knew that choices like "lose a few fingers or die" could be made.

He was able to control his mind to overcome tremendous pain and push fear aside. He *used* his fear to drive him toward success.

Freddie Chapman had Jedi-like abilities to control his mind, his thinking, his fears.

You can do the same thing.

What you do, how far you go, how much you succeed, what you achieve – they all come from your ability to control your mind. To control what you think about.

Where you end up in life comes down to something profoundly simple:

What you think about most is what you become.

You are today who you thought you would be. You will be in the future who you think you want to be today.

Everything in life – *everything* – starts with your thinking.

If you let fear drive your thoughts, you'll never do the tough things that lead to success.

You are actually a lot stronger than the fear in your mind lets you think you are.

Use your fear to push you toward positive activity – toward more creativity, more passion, more purpose.

If you want to dominate, control your thoughts, young Jedi.

BE EDGY
USE "JEDI MIND TRICKS" TO OUT THINK YOUR FEAR

1 **Keep your brain running at optimal levels.** Take care of yourself by getting plenty of rest and reducing stress so that excess cortisol doesn't cause permanent damage.

2 **Take control of your feelings.** Don't give in to the whimsy of how you're feeling at the time. Consciously talk yourself down from the fear that your amygdala and hippocampus use to keep you alive.

3 **Ask for a second opinion.** Ask someone you trust, "Does my perspective make sense?" Do this a few times, and you will start to see a pattern. You'll discover that when fear strikes, your perspective is completely different than when you are calm and in control.

4 **Take action right away.** Activity crushes fear. Do something. The bigger the better.

5 **Separate from negativity and force yourself to be positive.** A negative person is a mentally weak person. It takes no mental courage to have negative thoughts. What does take mental effort (sometimes lots of it) is to find the best in every situation. Make it a habit to stop negative beliefs and thinking. Force yourself to reframe negative experiences in a positive light. Consider every situation as an opportunity.

6 **Get logical.** Don't look at unpleasant circumstances as if "bad things always happen to me." When something unfortunate happens, view it simply as a problem to be solved rather than a reflection of your self-worth.

7 **Think in shades of gray.** Counter black-and-white thinking by considering all possibilities between two extremes. Rethink your own beliefs. Be open-minded.

THE POWER OF
LOVE

Any discussion about love in the context of success is sure to raise eyebrows.

We become instant skeptics when anyone tries to connect the idea of love with high performance.

Yet in sports we use the phrase "the love of the game" to separate good performance from extraordinary feats of greatness.

When two equally talented players go head to head, the winner is usually the one who loves the game more. We can feel it. We can see the effects of love right in front of us. We know it's real.

If we can spot the effects of love and marvel at its capacity to generate superstar performances, why are we so hesitant to accept love as a success differentiator in our own lives?

Because the idea of love conflicts with so much of what we think we understand about success.

We are told that feelings and love are distractions rather than motivators.

And so it's all too easy to dismiss love. To write it off.

Love is great for inspiring the hearts and souls of hurting people all over the world. But we struggle to embrace love in our own lives. We struggle to forgive and to nurture. To inspire. To make a difference.

There's no question that love is a challenging subject.

But before you start rolling your eyes at the idea of love as a success strategy or think about skipping ahead a few pages, hang with me.

After all, you picked up this book because you haven't yet achieved the level of success you want, right?

So let's talk about love.

We all want to be a better version of ourselves. That's why we set goals, go to the gym, try to eat healthy and generally try not to die too early. We are working toward something better.

That's why you're still reading this book. You want something more. So do I.

And wanting to be better, to be more, is a different discussion than just wanting to survive, right?

You have to do different things. You have to think differently.

When you really want something, when you really want to change, you look beyond ordinary behavior and tactics for something extraordinary.

That extra "something" you're looking for – believe it or not – is love.

Yes, love.

We call it a lot of things – kindness, empathy, compassion, selflessness – but it's really all the same thing.

Love.

It might not seem obvious at first that love is the answer. Frankly, it might seem preposterous even after thinking about it. Simply unbelievable.

And that's probably to be expected. In our quest for personal achievement, we've changed the conversation from what is magical to what is manageable.

Yet love is the most transformative power that we know.

It can do what no other attitude or emotion can achieve.

Love can bring your dream back to life.

And that's not just high-grade motivational mumbo-jumbo. It's been proven in the laboratory.

Quite literally, scientists have observed love bring dead brain matter back to life. The neurochemicals that are released in response to empathy and kindness, when sprinkled on dead brain cells, bring those cells back to life.

If the neurochemicals of love can revive dead cells, what could love do in your life? In your relationships?

Love is powerfully rehabilitating.

When you love others, you rehabilitate them.

When you love yourself, you rehabilitate you – you bring your hopes and dreams back to life. Scientists have also found a direct link between love and the health of the body's immune system. Love boosts your ability to heal yourself physically.

And emotionally.

Love unleashes powerful healing attitudes that force the brain to find the most optimistic perspective to any specific circumstance.

Think about a good memory from your past. Maybe a wedding, a graduation, time with your child or a stunning sunset. You remember a lot about that special moment. How it all happened. How you felt. Why it was so important to you.

But there are memories about that event that your brain has "helpfully" blocked out of your conscious memory.

Anything negative that doesn't jive with the emotion of that moment gets pushed to the background. Perhaps it was pouring down rain on your wedding day. Maybe the battery on your camera died during your son's kindergarten graduation.

But what you remember is how amazing that day was.

Love actively looks for only positive memories and serves them up as your first recollection of the event.

Love is why mothers remember only the joy surrounding the birth of their children and forget the pain.

Think about how transformational that is. You can actually heal your own pain by demonstrating love.

Physiologically, when you give or receive love, your brain is actually rewired. You think and act differently.

Love allows you to see the world and life in a new way, from a new perspective. It gives your brain a jolt of creativity that can help you transcend the problems that stand in the way of your success.

Love creates hope. Hope creates possibility. Possibility creates a context for success.

And yet, all this information about love isn't all that new. Deep down, you know all this instinctively.

Perhaps the scientific analysis is something you didn't know before. Perhaps the anecdotal health advantage is a novel perspective. But deep down in your soul, you know already that love is powerful.

That is why there is a part of each of us that is constantly in search of love. That's how we're wired. It's a subconscious longing all humans have. It's the silent motivation behind how we think and act.

We know how we feel when we love what we do. Not just working a job. But doing what we were meant to do.

We know how we feel when we're loved. We know how special, how confident, how secure we become when others show us love.

We know how fulfilled we are when we love others. Not just being in a relationship. But loving those we are with.

And, we know what it's like to not be loved. We know the agony of love that is torn from us. We know the deep hurt of losing love, losing friendships. It's a silent agony that can bring even the strongest person to their knees.

Love makes a simple loss something we feel deeply. But it also adds depth to our successes.

To love is to live with purpose and passion.

I have found that most of us need more love in our lives.

I know I do. Maybe you do, too.

Helen Keller once made an ironically insightful observation: *"The best and most beautiful things in the world cannot be seen or even touched. They must be felt with the heart."*

If a blind and deaf woman can understand the impact of love, how much more should we be able to when we can see it all around us?

You may know the story of Michael Oher from the book or movie about his life. Even so, it bears repeating.

Michael was born in one of the poorest parts of Memphis, TN. His mother was a crack cocaine addict and an alcoholic; his father spent more time in jail than as a free man. One of 12 children, Michael was left to fend for himself. No love. No care. Just survival. One day at a time.

Child services placed him in foster care at the age of seven. But even there he was an afterthought. He received little attention and no discipline. He failed first grade and had to repeat it. The same thing happened in second grade. During his first nine years as a student, he attended 11 different schools.

That's how Michael spent his childhood. A statistic. A failure. A poor black kid that the world looked down on. Shuffled from foster home to foster home, he often ran away. He preferred to be homeless. And he was only a child.

But then compassion, kindness and love changed Michael's life forever.

Tony Henderson, the father of one of Michael's friends who lived outside the projects, regularly let Michael sleep on his couch. When Tony took his son Steven to be enrolled in Briarcrest Christian Academy, an elite private school, he took Michael along. Tony spoke to the school's football coach, who ultimately convinced the headmaster to give Michael a chance.

Then, Sean Tuohy, whose daughter Collins was in one of Michael's classes, noticed Michael hanging around the school gym and made an effort to get to know him. He soon realized Michael had no money and started paying for his lunches. That November, Sean's wife, Leigh Anne, was driving past a bus stop near the school when she saw Michael get off the bus in a T-shirt and jeans but no coat. She took him shopping for some clothes and invited him for Thanksgiving.

Over time, the Tuohys welcomed Michael into their home. They paid his tuition to Briarcrest. They hired a private tutor to help him fix his failing grades. They gave him his own room and bought him a new wardrobe.

But the Tuohys went beyond giving money and help. They sincerely cared about Michael. And he became a part of their family.

A little over a year later, Leigh Anne told Michael something he had never heard before: *"I love you."* It was a statement that Michael would never forget. Shortly after that, the Tuohys became his adoptive parents. The Tuohy children – Collins and S.J. – were some of his best friends and biggest cheerleaders.

Michael continued to thrive with the Tuohys. He lettered in track, basketball and football and was named one of the top offensive linemen in the country. Recruited by college football programs all over the country, he accepted a scholarship to play football at the University of Mississippi. He became an All American his freshman year and went on to win almost every award for his position in college football.

In April 2009, Michael was selected in the first round of the NFL draft by the Baltimore Ravens, signing a contract for almost $14 million. And the Tuohys were right there with him.

It was love that made the difference.

Real love. Real compassion. Real caring.

No plan, no strategy, no amount of money could replace what kindness and compassion could inspire.

Love is transformational. Nothing can completely change a situation like love can.

If you've read this far, then you're probably in agreement with me that there is something to this love thing. If you aren't completely convinced, then you're at least giving me the benefit of the doubt. I'll take it.

And then I'll challenge you to really think about what you call love.

I'd be willing to bet that some of what you call love isn't really love at all. It's passive-aggressive behavior.

See, the downside of love is that you can get hurt. Badly.

Real love is hard. It's risky. It sucks sometimes.

You can love others deeply and be taken advantage of. You can be betrayed and lied to.

That's tough to handle. So painful that your subconscious kick-starts your natural defense mechanisms against getting hurt: being passive aggressive.

You invest in what looks like love, but underneath it's full of trapdoors in case you need to get out in a hurry. You want to make sure that if anybody is going to lose, it's the other person and not you.

Passive aggression isn't just a little bit different than love. It's completely different.

Love tries to help. Passive aggression tries to look helpful.

Love keeps you focused on others. Passive aggression keeps you focused on what others think of you.

Love is forgiving. Passive aggression never forgets.

Love is sympathetic. Passive aggression is cynical.

Love is nurturing. Passive aggression is needy.

Love is patient. Passive aggression is petty.

Love is giving. Passive aggression is giving in order to get.

With passive aggression, how you act may look like love, but how you think is completely different.

Now don't get defensive if this touches a raw nerve...but if you find yourself having to defend why and how you are a loving person, yet you never experience the benefits of being a loving person, then you might have a problem.

You have to judge yourself. I can't do that for you.

You have to look deep within. You have to ask yourself hard questions about your attitude and your motivations and figure out what drives you.

This whole book has been about confronting and fixing the behaviors and attitudes that limit your ability to be amazing. If you aren't careful, passive aggression will rob you of your dreams and goals and inspiration.

You can't replace the transformational power of love with the transactional nature of passive aggression.

At times, they might look the same, but they drive completely different results.

One leads to a better you. The other leads to a bitter you.

If you want to be transformed, you need to think differently about love.

You've got to have a human strategy to succeed in life.

Love is the foundation of a human strategy. It is the lifeblood, the inspiration, that enables everything else to work.

You know that pain and fear drive people. You can use that knowledge to manipulate them.

Or you can understand their insecurities and fears and counterbalance them with love.

Love is the foundation of real change, real progress, real relationships.

Love is a sustainable long-term strategy. It is the one thing that works in every situation.

And it is one of the few differences you can actually achieve *right now. Today.*

Do you want to be extraordinary? Love more.

When you love more, you do more. You can't help it.

You change the possibilities for your future when you love. Despite the pain in your life right now. Despite the fear that you are feeling.

Love allows you to see the opportunity behind the obstacles.

Love allows you to admit failure and forces you to keep trying.

Love allows you to invest in the greatness of others.

Love allows you to connect with the suffering and desires of others.

Love allows you to deliver outrageous acts of kindness.

Love allows others to care about you and your success.

So choose love.

Love the work you do.

Love the people around you.

Love that you are making a difference.

And always love more than you think you need to.

BE EDGY
LOVE MORE

1 Be vulnerable. While it is difficult to put yourself in positions where you might get emotionally hurt, it's also one of the best places for potential opportunities to find you. When you genuinely care about others and they feel that you are approachable, they will reach out to you. They will want to help you succeed.

2 Be honest. If you're already hurting or have hurt those around you, it's all too easy to hide from the truth. But you're probably just lying to yourself. And lying and loving can't exist together in the same lifestyle. To learn how to love, you have to be brutally honest with yourself about your own limitations and what you can improve.

3 Be purposeful. Intentionally plan to impact the lives of others. That means going out of your way to be generous and thoughtful. You don't wait for someone to trip and fall and then run to lift them up. You look around and actively encourage those who might be suffering silently.

CHOOSE TO BE
EXTRAORDINARY

EDGY is a roadmap to outrageous success for ordinary people like you and me.

Doing what seems extreme. Being disciplined enough to give yourself a chance to succeed. Going further than anyone around you thinks is safe or acceptable. Giving when it hurts most. Learning how to love in spite of pain and fear.

EDGY is your way forward.

It's what you can start doing right now. It's who you can become.

And yet, you can want to be EDGY, but never do it. Never become it.

Because EDGY doesn't just happen.

Being extraordinary doesn't just happen.

Doing something amazing isn't an accident.

Living an extraordinary life doesn't come naturally.

What comes naturally is to just be ordinary.

And that is how most of us stay. Ordinary. Average. Mediocre.

Active yet ineffective. Moving...but not toward our dreams.

Being ordinary is a bad plan. Pursuing the path of least resistance means high-grade mediocrity and close-but-not-quite-there results.

Mediocrity is an effective (and frustrating) villain.

145

It is neither crashing defeat nor breathtaking failure. But a slow, soul-sucking poison. A silent assassin.

One minute you're standing on top of the world. The next you're at the bottom of the heap, scratching your head and wondering what happened.

You've completely lost your mojo. And you're not even sure how you got to this awful place called mediocrity.

And more than anything else, you want your mojo back. You want that confidence, that feeling of control, that ability to perform at high levels.

You want to do more, be more.

There is a word for that. A word to describe something that transcends mediocrity. A word that communicates "more than average."

Extra-ordinary.

Not ordinary. Something extra.

But how does extraordinary happen?

Extraordinary starts with you – perhaps an ordinary person at an ordinary job doing ordinary things on an ordinary day.

No special advantages. No remarkable skills that can't be duplicated. No large bank account.

Just all-around *"ordinary."*

Then, you decide to do something extra. To be something extra. Something a lot-a-bit extra.

And not just one time. But day after day after day.

And then one day, everyone watching you will notice that *"ordinary"* is no longer an accurate description for the person you have become. For what you have done.

And they will shake their heads and remark that what they have seen is extraordinary.

Because it was. And because you will be.

And that's how extraordinary happens.

By not being satisfied with ordinary.

By being vigilant. Being obsessed.

No excuses. Just a relentless focus on being better.

It's deciding to go the extra mile when the last mile was hard enough. It's controlling your mind in spite of the obstacles ahead.

It comes down to this really simple thought: If you don't make time to pursue being extraordinary, then you'll never experience true greatness. All you'll ever know is mediocrity.

You're already making time to be average and ordinary.

Why not aim for extraordinary?

Make no mistake...avoiding mediocrity and becoming extraordinary will be more challenging than you ever imagined.

But you can do just about anything when you decide that what you want is worth fighting for, worth living for.

In July 2007, superstar chef Grant Achatz shocked the culinary world with the news that he had Stage 4 cancer in his mouth. More specifically, his tongue. With such an advanced stage, doctors told him the only way to stay alive was to

remove almost all of his tongue. But that wasn't something Grant was willing to accept.

You see, all that Grant had ever dreamed about was being a chef.

Since his earliest days working in his parents' restaurant in Michigan, he had pursued acceptance to the prestigious Culinary Institute of America. After graduation, he worked his way up to sous chef at the celebrated restaurant

French Laundry in California and then became Executive Chef for the four-star Trio in Chicago. Three years later, with Grant leading the restaurant, Trio was awarded a fifth star, making it one of only 13 restaurants in the world with that distinction.

And then Grant did the unthinkable. He left Trio at the peak of worldwide acclaim to start his own restaurant, Alinea.

A block from Chicago's famous Steppenwolf Theatre Company, Alinea was located in a simple brick building with no sign, just a number above the door. It had no bar, no lobby or waiting area, and just enough room for five dozen diners. Less than two years later, his creation was rated five stars by Mobil and named the best restaurant in America by *Gourmet* Magazine.

It was at the height of his success that Grant was diagnosed with cancer. The prognosis was grim. Doctors told him the cancer had likely already spread to his lymph nodes. Removing most of his tongue gave him the best chance for survival.

But Grant decided to go a different direction.

He underwent chemotherapy and radiation. He chose experimental procedures under the watchful eyes of leading doctors at the University of Chicago. He was so sick that he would vomit during the brief car ride to his restaurant. The radiation stripped layers of delicate skin off his swollen tongue and throat. For weeks he could barely swallow anything. He completely lost his sense of taste. More importantly, he was close to losing his life.

Despite his pain and fear and desire to not have other people feel sorry for him, Grant decided to do whatever it took to keep his dream alive, to keep himself alive. He poured what little energy he had into creating culinary mastery. To cook, he had another chef taste his food and describe in intricate detail the flavors he was creating. He developed an extraordinary sense of smell and started to rely more on the nuances of smell and color to create an extraordinary dining experience.

It would be months before he started to get his sense of taste back. Sweets were the first thing he could taste again. And as the tissue on the rest of his tongue continued to regrow, he started to sense salty and sour.

In December 2007, when doctors looked at scans of Grant's mouth and throat, the cancer was gone. And so a week before Christmas, Grant announced that his cancer was in remission.

But there's more to the story. In 2008, Alinea was rated in the top 25 restaurants in the world; then 10th in the world in 2009. By 2010, Grant's dream was the highest-rated restaurant in North America and seventh in the world and earned a coveted three stars from *The Michelin Guide*.

Grant Achatz might not be alive now if he had chosen to be ordinary. If he had decided to be a victim, accept his fate and live the rest of his life as a casualty.

Had he done that, he likely wouldn't have a world-famous restaurant and a legacy of creativity, culinary design and inspiration.

Instead, he chose to be extraordinary.

And that mindset is a choice.

It's a personal transformation from excuses and self-pity to passion and purpose.

And so instead of gathering around his tombstone and talking about what a great guy he was, people talk about who Grant *is*. And what greater things he still might do.

And while you might not have to fight cancer to help you define how much you want your destiny, every day – a dozen times each day – you choose your reaction to life.

Every moment is a choice to pursue what is most important or to make an excuse and run away from making the hard decisions.

Career decisions, relationship decisions, health decisions, life decisions.

You have the choice to give in to the fear that consumes you or to stand up and make your mark on the world.

The key to being extraordinary is living in the *now*.

Now is the time to start working on the future you want.

Now is your chance to decide what tomorrow will look like.

Now is your opportunity to do the things that scare you the most.

Now is the best time to keep going.

Now is when you need to stop and think about others.

Now is your chance to develop new skills.

Now is when your dreams begin to turn into reality.

Now. *Right now.*

You see, at this very moment, you are at a crossroads.

Right now, you decide the ending to your life story.

And you'll be at this same crossroads a few more times today, tomorrow and every day for the rest of your life.

The secret to getting what you want from life is understanding that what you do *right now* drives your future.

You can put off doing what is important, or you can start working on it right now.

That's your choice to make.

You can blame your procrastination on slick language around "priorities" and "potential." But you know the truth.

You can be extraordinary.

Starting *now*.

It's never too late to do something amazing.

It's never too early to start trying.

Consider the following:

At age 1, Christian Friedrich Heinecken, the legendary child prodigy, had read the Pentateuch (the first five books of the Bible).

At 2, speed skater Bonnie Blair began skating. She would go on to win five Olympic gold medals.

At 3, Wolfgang Mozart taught himself to play the harpsichord.

At 4, Brazilian Formula One race car driver Ayrton Senna da Silva began driving.

At 5, Yo-Yo Ma, world-famous cellist, began playing "Suites for Unaccompanied Cello" before bed each evening.

At 6, Willie Hoppe, the greatest billiards player in history, began to play pool. He had to stand on a box to reach the table.

At 7, English philosopher and economist John Stuart Mill had mastered Greek.

At 8, three-time Olympic gold medal runner Wilma Rudolph took her first step after suffering from polio as a child.

At 9, Daisy Ashford wrote her bestselling novel, *The Young Visiters*. It sold over 200,000 copies.

At 10, Vinay Bhat became the youngest chess master in the world.

At 11, pilot Victoria Van Meter became the youngest girl to fly across the United States.

At 12, Carl von Clausewitz, general and writer of *On War*, joined the Prussian army.

At 13, actress, director and producer Jodie Foster wrote and directed a short movie called *The Hands of Time*.

At 14, Romanian gymnast Nadia Comaneci became the first athlete in Olympic history to achieve a perfect 10.

At 15, Swedish tennis star Bjorn Borg dropped out of school to concentrate on tennis.

At **16**, American sharpshooter Annie Oakley challenged and defeated the well-known marksman Frank Butler by hitting a dime in midair from 90 feet.

At **17**, soccer legend Pele won the World Cup for Brazil and then passed out on the field.

At **18**, Norwegian mathematician Niels Henrik Abel proved that it was impossible to solve the general equation of fifth degree by algebraic means.

At **19**, Abner Doubleday devised the rules for baseball.

At **20**, Charles Lindbergh learned to fly.

At **21**, Thomas Edison created his first invention, an electric vote recorder.

At **22**, Olympic runner Herbert James Elliott, one of the greatest mile runners ever, retired undefeated.

At **23**, English poet Jane Taylor wrote "Twinkle, Twinkle, Little Star."

At **24**, Ted Turner took over his father's billboard advertising business. He later launched cable news network CNN.

At **25**, Janis Joplin made her first recording, "Cheap Thrills," which grossed over $1 million within a few months.

At **26**, Soviet cosmonaut Valentina Tereshkova became the first woman to travel in space.

At **27**, Kurt Vonnegut, Jr. left his job at General Electric to become a full-time writer.

At **28**, Jamaican reggae composer/performer Bob Marley recorded "I Shot the Sheriff."

At **29**, Scottish-born inventor Alexander Graham Bell transmitted the first complete sentence by telephone.

At **30**, physicist Armand Fizeau measured the speed of light.

At **31**, French Egyptologist Jean-François Champollion deciphered the Rosetta stone.

At **32**, Alexander the Great had conquered almost the entire known world.

At 33, Walter Nilsson rode across the United States on an 8-ft. unicycle.

At 34, Francis Scott Key, after witnessing the bombardment of Fort McHenry, wrote "The Star-Spangled Banner."

At 35, Sir Frederick William Herschel, an English astronomer, invented the contact lens.

At 36, Barthelemy Thimonnier developed the world's first practical sewing machine.

At 37, Jersey Joe Walcott became the oldest man ever to win the world heavyweight boxing title.

At 38, Apollo 11 commander Neil Armstrong became the first person to set foot on the moon.

At 39, Sharon Sites Adams became the first woman to sail alone across the Pacific Ocean.

At 40, Hank Aaron hit his 715th home run.

At 41, Rudyard Kipling became the youngest Nobel Prize Laureate in literature.

At 42, Kareem Abdul-Jabbar became the oldest regular NBA player.

At 43, baseball player Nolan Ryan pitched the sixth no-hitter of his career.

At 44, George Washington crossed the Delaware River and captured Trenton, NJ.

At 45, Andre Marie Ampere, a French physicist, discovered the rules relating magnetic fields and electric currents.

At 46, Jack Nicklaus became the oldest golfer ever to win the Masters.

At 47, Kent Couch attached 105 helium balloons to a lawn chair and flew 193 miles.

At 48, Umberto Eco, a professor of semiotics, wrote his first novel, *The Name of the Rose*.

At 49, Julia Child published her book, *Mastering the Art of French Cooking.*

At 50, P.L. Guinand, a Swiss inventor, patented a new method for making optical glass.

At 51, The Marquis de Sade, imprisoned for much of his life, wrote the novel *Justine*.

At 52, Sir Francis Chichester sailed around the world alone in a 53-foot boat normally manned by a crew of six.

At 53, Walter Hunt, an inventor, patented the safety pin.

At 54, Annie Jump Cannon became the first astronomer to classify the stars according to spectral type.

At 55, Pablo Picasso completed his masterpiece, "Guernica."

At 56, Mao Zedong founded the People's Republic of China.

At 57, Frank Dobesh competed in his first 100-mile bicycle ride – exactly 10 years after he was diagnosed with an inoperable brain tumor.

At 58, Sony chairman Akio Morita introduced the Sony Walkman, an idea no one seemed to like at the time.

At 59, "Satchel" Paige became the oldest Major League baseball player.

At 60, playwright and essayist George Bernard Shaw finished writing *Heartbreak House*, regarded by many as his masterpiece.

At 61, Charles Cagniard de la Tour, a French doctor, demonstrated that fermentation depends upon yeast cells.

At 62, J.R.R. Tolkien published the first volume of his fantasy series, *Lord of the Rings*.

At 63, John Dryden undertook the enormous task of translating the entire works of Virgil into English verse.

At 64, Thomas Bowdler "bowdlerized" Shakespeare's works, making them "family friendly."

At 65, jazz musician Miles Davis defiantly performed his final live album, just weeks before he died.

At 66, Noah Webster completed his monumental *American Dictionary of the English Language*.

At 67, Simeon Poisson discovered the laws of probability after studying the likelihood of death from mule kicks in the French army.

At 68, the English experimentalist Sir William Crookes began investigating radioactivity and invented a device for detecting alpha particles.

At 69, Canadian Ed Whitlock of Milton, Ontario, Canada, became the oldest person to run a standard marathon in under three hours (2:52:47).

At 70, Cornelius Vanderbilt began buying railroads.

At 71, Katsusuke Yanagisawa, a retired Japanese schoolteacher, became the oldest person to climb Mt. Everest.

At 72, Margaret Ringenberg flew around the world.

At 73, Larry King celebrated his 50th year in broadcasting.

At 74, Ferdinand Marie de Lesseps began an attempt to construct the Suez Canal.

At 75, cancer survivor Barbara Hillary became one of the oldest people, and the first black woman, to reach the North Pole.

At 76, Arthur Miller unveiled a bold new play, *The Ride Down Mt. Morgan,* free of the world-weary tone of his previous works.

At 77, John Glenn became the oldest person to go into space.

At 78, Chevalier de Lamarck proposed a new theory of the evolutionary process, claiming that acquired characteristics can be transmitted to offspring.

At 79, Asa Long became the oldest U.S. checkers champion.

At 80, Christine Brown of Laguna Hills, CA, flew to China and climbed the Great Wall.

At 81, Bill Painter became the oldest person to reach the 14,411-foot summit of Mt. Rainier.

At 82, William Ivy Baldwin became the oldest tightrope walker, crossing the South Boulder Canyon in Colorado on a 320-foot wire.

At 83, famed baby doctor Benjamin Spock championed for world peace.

At 84, W. Somerset Maugham wrote *Points of View.*

At 85, Theodor Mommsen became the oldest person to receive a Nobel Prize in Literature.

At 86, Katherine Pelton swam the 200-meter butterfly in 3 minutes, 1.14 seconds, beating the men's world record for that age group by over 20 seconds.

At 87, Mary Baker Eddy founded the *Christian Science Monitor.*

At 88, Michelangelo created the architectural plans for the Church of Santa Maria degli Angeli.

At 89, Arthur Rubinstein performed one of his greatest recitals in Carnegie Hall.

At 90, Marc Chagall became the first living artist to be exhibited at the Louvre museum.

At 91, Allan Stewart of New South Wales completed a Bachelor of Law degree from the University of New England.

At 92, Paul Spangler finished his 14th marathon.

At 93, P.G. Wodehouse worked on his 97th novel, was knighted and died.

At 94, comedian George Burns performed in Schenectady, NY, 63 years after his first performance there.

At 95, Nola Ochs became the oldest person to receive a college diploma.

At 96, Harry Bernstein published his first book, *The Invisible Wall*, three years after he started writing to cope with loneliness after his wife of 70 years, Ruby, passed away.

At 97, Martin Miller was still working fulltime as a lobbyist on behalf of benefits for seniors.

At 98, Beatrice Wood, a ceramist, exhibited her latest work.

At 99, Teiichi Igarashi climbed Mt. Fuji.

At 100, Frank Schearer seems to be the oldest active water skier in the world.

People are doing extraordinary things all the time. And there's no reason you can't be one of those people.

But never forget that "doing" is only half the battle.

The person you become is where true success lies.

In the end, we all want to believe that who we are matters. We are made to search for meaning – to find self-worth, self-fulfillment.

Like footprints through the timeline of destiny, we like to look back and feel assured that our being here has made the world a better place. We desperately want to know that we made a difference.

See, you can only *do* so much. But you can *be* a difference 100 times today.

And just think about what could happen if you chose to be that difference 100 times every day for the next year...you would have hundreds of thousands of small opportunities to make an impact.

Now imagine if you did that for the next 30 years...you could change over a million outcomes for the better.

Now that would be truly extraordinary.

Choose to be EDGY.

Choose to be extraordinary.

BE EDGY
CHOOSE TO BE EXTRAORDINARY

1. Open the door for a stranger
2. Say, "Thank you"
3. Learn from your mistakes
4. Stop whining
5. Fear less
6. Be kind
7. Let yourself be inspired
8. Lead someone
9. Pay off debt
10. Choose a side
11. Pay more for quality
12. Lend a hand
13. Let past mistakes go
14. Be invincible
15. Be more efficient with your time
16. Stop playing politics
17. Plan to be successful
18. Be an expert
19. Stop defending yourself
20. Decide to take action today
21. Fight mediocrity
22. Laugh at life
23. Go to bed tired
24. Ask what you can do better
25. Give a stranger flowers
26. Hold the elevator door
27. Compliment a great idea
28. Work on being patient
29. Create what's missing
30. Stay in mental shape
31. Practice getting back up
32. Shake hands while looking the other person in the eye

33. Assume the best in others
34. Try something new
35. Listen to your critics
36. Get into financial shape
37. Donate time to charity
38. Teach what you've learned
39. Give an opinion when it's hard
40. Care about others
41. Pay attention to the details
42. Be a friend
43. Do physical labor
44. Brag on someone else
45. Share more
46. Love someone
47. Have a dream
48. Get up an hour earlier
49. Write down your thoughts
50. Apologize more
51. Stay mentally strong
52. Put yourself in tough places
53. Cry when you are hurt
54. Have a purpose each day
55. Don't stop until you finish
56. Be passionate about others
57. Pay attention to the conversation
58. Appreciate differences
59. Be less selfish
60. Ease someone else's pain
61. Imagine the possibilities
62. Smile at those around you
63. Care enough to cry
64. Make a call just because you're thinking about them

65. Be a mentor

66. Fail gracefully

67. Practice being vulnerable

68. Decide to be optimistic

69. Ask more questions

70. Read a new biography

71. Do something outrageous

72. Think for yourself

73. Put in more effort

74. Ask for help

75. Tell the truth

76. Get some exercise

77. Decide not to get angry

78. Explore new ideas

79. Be more effective with your talents

80. Slow down (for a few minutes)

81. Pursue your goals each day

82. Make a list of tasks to get done

83. Live with honor

84. Feed your inspiration

85. Avoid the crowd

86. Stop being passive aggressive

87. Find answers to your questions

88. Be accountable

89. Work on your biggest weakness

90. Replace "No" with "No thanks"

91. Let someone else get the attention

92. Listen with your eyes

93. Say what's on your mind

94. Defend your friends

95. Shake off the straws before they break your back

96. Offer encouragement

97. Meditate on your goals

98. Don't do anything halfway

99. Do good things for the right reasons

100. Get help for your head

101. Demand brutal analysis of your actions

102. Put in the effort you expect of others

103. Share a good example

104. Offer to buy dinner or dessert

105. Decide to learn from everyone

106. Make a big deal of small wins

107. Let life happen around you

108. Have a big vision for those around you

109. Enjoy others' success

110. Inspire others quietly

111. Deliberately invest in healing

112. Welcome diverse perspectives

113. Don't go to bed angry

114. Anticipate the success of others

115. Value your own time

116. Ask others to "pay it forward"

117. Write a kind note

118. Offer to help for free

119. Have a plan

120. Overlook immaturity

121. Care less about being right

122. Schedule time to invest in others

123. Give away your best idea

124. Stop being offended so easily

125. Remember the good times

126. Decide that caring is more important than winning

FIGHT **UNTIL THE END**

At what point does your dream become delusion?

Who decides when genius is just plain insanity?

The world doesn't get to tell you when to stop fighting for your dream.

Friends and family will shake their heads and wonder why you're trying so hard.

They will ask you to stop.

They will tell you that you're throwing your life away.

They will tell you that you're wrong.

They will tell you that even if you get what you want, it won't be worth the cost.

Small visions and petty mindsets don't help your mission or further your cause. They just hold you back and make you doubt your purpose and passion.

You might be called crazy or fanatical or obsessive. But so were a lot of other amazing people throughout history.

If you let the opinions of others dictate what you do and how you feel about your life, you are destined to be miserable no matter how much you accomplish.

Success is what *you* decide it is. Not what other people tell you it should be.

Don't let other people's opinions define you. Their opinions don't matter. Not one little bit.

They don't get to decide.

You do.

You decide what is right for you and what is wrong. You decide how important your goals and dreams are to you. You decide how long to keep trying.

There will be times when the world seems to fall apart around you. When everything you try seems to fail. When your dreams are in tatters, and what you want seems so distant and unreachable that it might as well be a fairytale.

There will be quiet moments in between the gasps of a silent sob when you question if you can go on.

When no one believes in you. Not even you.

In those dark moments, it's only natural that you would think about giving up.

You start quitting on the inside.

That's where quitting starts. In your head. In your heart.

Think about it. When was the last time you publicly "threw in the towel"? Probably only once or twice ever.

We've been taught that quitting is for losers – that successful people don't give up. And since we all want to look like winners, we work hard at making sure we don't ever appear to give up.

But giving up isn't about what you do when everyone is watching you.

It's about the attitude you have, the things you say to yourself, when you're faced with overwhelming obstacles.

You give up because you don't believe in you enough. Because when no one else believes in you, you suspect they're right.

When others doubt you, you doubt yourself, too. When others are skeptical of your dreams, you become skeptical of your dreams, too.

You fail only if you quit.

You will succeed if you just won't quit.

Success looks a lot like failure up until the moment you break through the finish line.

You can give up or keep shuffling toward your goal one step at a time.

You can make excuses for your own inadequacies, or you can take responsibility for achieving greatness.

Today could be the day you start winning.

Just because things didn't go your way the first time – or any time so far – doesn't mean that they won't go your way the next time.

The next time could be the time you win.

The next time could be the time when the human spirit rises above the beliefs of frail minds to deliver results that could never have been imagined.

But only if you believe. Only if you believe in you.

No one else can believe for you or with you or instead of you.

It has to be you.

You need undying devotion to making your dreams reality.

You need purpose.

You need conviction.

In the summer of 480 B.C., Xerxes and his Persian army descended on the plains of Greece with a force that shook the world. Their goal: to invade and enslave Greece. Ancient sources claim the Persian army numbered in the millions. And their ferocity was indisputable. They would not be denied.

And yet a single man dared question that greatness.

As Greece and its allies struggled to assemble several

thousand men to mount a defense, Leonidas I, King of Sparta, gathered a small group of men in the hopes of delaying the Persian army long enough to give Greece a chance. Leonidas and his men made their way through the night to a pass in the mountains called Thermopylae, through which the Persians had to pass to reach the Greek towns.

The following morning, as hundreds of thousands of Persians charged their position, the Spartans stood their ground - unmoved, unshaken. They stood with purpose, shoulder to shoulder, brother with brother. Willing to die for their country. Fighting to live. Leonidas leading.

According to an account by Herodotus, "Leonidas required them to stand firm – to conquer or die." And their fury drove back the Persians. That day and the next and then again for five more days.

Seven days into the battle, a Greek traitor named Ephialtes informed the Persians about a little-known path through the mountains – a way around the pass that Leonidas held with his men. Hearing this, Xerxes ordered Hydarnes and 10,000 elite soldiers called the Immortals to ascend the mountain at night and outflank the Spartans.

When dawn came and the Greek scouts spotted the Immortals, they reported the treachery to Leonidas. Knowing that death was likely, he gathered his small army and announced that anyone who wished to leave was permitted to go with honor. Those who remained would fight the Persians to the death.

As daylight broke across the top of the hills, the small army of only 300 Spartans formed a circle and waited for the enemy. As the Persians surrounded them, the Spartans fought so fiercely that their opponents "fell in heaps."

The Persian commanders were forced to use whips to drive their soldiers at the Spartans, who fought with violent desperation, their swords breaking against the heavy shields of the Immortals.

And yet they fought on.

As wave after endless wave of Persians descended upon the valiant troop, Leonidas was separated from his men and killed – his hand still grasping the sword his lifeless body could no longer command.

His troops, so moved by his passing, were enraged and fought the Persians back up the hill to surround their fallen king's body. They stood in a circle, facing outward, fighting to the last with their swords. And when their swords broke, so Herodotus tells us, they fought with their hands and teeth. Nothing left but sheer will and a determination to stand. Nothing left but conviction.

Ultimately, it took the arrows of thousands of Persian archers raining down on the Spartans to crush them. None were left standing. Their bodies lay fallen around Leonidas – a man who stood up to the mighty Xerxes. A man against millions. A man who believed in his cause. A man who pushed aside comfort, fear and a kingdom to pursue his destiny.

So inspired were the Greeks by the courage and conviction of Leonidas and his 300 Spartans that they rose up as a nation. They fought to be free men and, against staggering odds, defeated the Persians. And in so doing, they ensured the birth of Western democracy and freedom.

One man literally and truly changed the course of history.

To this day, there is a memorial to Leonidas and his men at Thermopylae. Engraved upon a stone is Leonidas' response to Xerxes' demand that the Spartans lay down their arms: "Molon labe"..."Come and take them."

Thousands of years ago, in a battle between primal warriors, to lose meant death.

The choice was brutally clear.

And so, no matter how badly you were injured, you fought on. You grabbed your weapon and with every ounce of strength you could muster, you waged war with the enemy.

Chances are that fighting for your dream is a lot easier than raising a sword and fighting hand-to-hand to the death.

But fighting to achieve your goals is a raw and gritty sport. It can leave you bloodied, hurt and wondering why you ever attempted such grand ambitions in the first place.

Giving up on your dream is likely not a life-and-death situation. At least not a physical one.

But the moment you stop fighting for it, you start dying inside.

When you give up, you die an emotional death.

Do you have the guts and the stamina and the conviction to keep fighting for your dream?

Because if you aren't fighting, you just aren't getting any closer to success. You aren't.

So grab your sword and start swinging.

When you are grimacing through the pain and fatigue of fighting for what you hold most dear, remember the Spartan inside you.

Meet the challenge with the noble nod of a warrior. The steady look of an unconquerable champion.

And when fear and doubt surround you, fight!

Fight furiously!

Fight for the dignity of a destiny that you choose.

And if you should fall, rise.

Dust off the wounds of failure and loss.

And try again. And then try again and again and again.

Don't throw up your hands, hang your head and admit defeat.

Refuse to lose quietly.

Because your dream is worth fighting for.

You have a choice. A choice to give up or to fight on.

This moment is pivotal.

This moment defines the rest of your life. This moment is your opportunity to believe in yourself.

One person is enough to change history.

That person might be you.

Will you stand and fight?

EPILOGUE
THE REST OF THE STORY

Do you remember George?

George was the young American soldier caught in World War II who pulled himself, broken and bleeding, in excruciating pain and at the brink of death, across a battlefield to find help.

Then he overcame his fears and swam through a pitch-black ocean in the dark of night in hopes of finding a boat where doctors and nurses could begin to make him whole.

It was extreme. It was improbable. But George survived.

And I'm glad he did.

Because George was George Waldschmidt – my grandfather.

But George didn't just survive. He became successful. In a big way. In an EDGY kind of way.

After the war, he moved to Kansas, started a family and drove a train as an engineer.

Nothing glamorous. Nothing especially heroic.

In fact, if the story stopped there, you might suspect that George was just an average blue-collar worker for the rest of his life.

But the same drive that enabled George to pull himself back from the edge of death enabled him to become a millionaire. A millionaire train engineer.

You see, at the end of each year, Western Pacific employees were given the option of receiving a cash bonus or a stock certificate. In those days, a stock certificate was just a piece of paper that let you know you might have some money in something called the stock market in New York City.

Although most of his fellow engineers took the cash, George took the stock.

Instead of giving in to immediate gratification, he demonstrated a savvy discipline that seemed extreme to those he drank beer with. So while others were paying for another round at the bar or buying a new house, George kept collecting pieces of paper.

And over the course of many years, those little pieces of paper made George a millionaire several times over.

During the 20 years that I knew my grandfather, I was always inspired by his story. It would pop back into the forefront of my mind whenever I was facing challenges.

How could I not put in the effort or be disciplined knowing what my grandfather had done?

Now, to be fair, George's journey wasn't all inspiring. He had his demons.

Like many of his generation who fought battles on faraway continents, he used alcohol as an escape from the horrors he had witnessed and the tragedy he had experienced.

He was abusive at times. Angry. Out of control.

But my grandmother loved him in spite of it. Her commitment to him was a testament to the power of love.

Because when it's all said and done, it is the love and the relationships in our lives that mean so much more than any other kind of success.

I learned that lesson in the most painful of ways.

And that's where we were at the beginning of this book...

With me, sitting on the back steps of my garage with a gun in my mouth, having discovered in no uncertain terms that I'd been wrong. That achieving outrageous, extraordinary success in life wasn't about how many deals I closed, how much money I made or who knew my name.

It was about something much deeper than that.

There are few words to accurately describe the emotional torment of my failed marriage. I was distraught at a deeply personal level. Hurt. Confused. Incredibly sad.

There were few days that I didn't think about committing suicide. But once I put the gun down that night, I was never again really serious about hurting myself.

But the thought would still go through my mind, "Wouldn't it just be easier to end it all than to try to put the pieces back together?"

Perhaps it would have been.

But that's not how we Waldschmidts do things.

Just as my grandfather crawled off the battlefield an inch at a time, my wife and I learned how to stop hurting each other, bit by bit.

We learned that we both just wanted to be loved. To be listened to. To know that we mattered.

Like George, we found help. We found each other.

And like George, we survived.

Sara and I are still together today. This year we will have been married for 10 years. And we have three amazing children.

Don't expect any advice from me on how to keep a marriage together. We just took it day by day. And the days turned into weeks. The weeks turned into months. The months turned into years.

And now, we love each other more than ever. Perhaps truly for the first time.

I don't know what the future holds for us, but I'm excited to find out.

And I'm grateful for a grandfather who inspired me to find the courage to conquer my demons and do the impossible.

My hope for you is that you will find the courage to conquer your own demons, whatever they may be.

To push the limits of what is safe and acceptable.

To keep fighting long after it makes sense to stop.

To give to others more than feels necessary.

To understand the frailty of others.

And to love them in spite of it.

Go be awesome.
Go be EDGY.

THANKS

There has been so much love in my life. My wife, Sara, is my rock. Nothing else matters as long as I have her. Together we will conquer the world. Bryce and Dustin and Dylan are the reason that I am writing this book. I hope when they are old enough to read a book like this they will understand how much I love them and want them to be extraordinary people.

Dad and Mom Waldschmidt started this craziness. I have to give them credit for lighting a fire under me. They taught me how to conquer, to love Jesus and to be my own man. My dad showed me the beauty of the open road and a pair of running shoes.

Thanks, Terry, for being a second dad to me. Kyle, Liz, Paul, Katy, Faith, Joy, Joe, Jeremy, Brenda, Ricky, Cassie, Hannah, Rich, Nicholas, Lisa – no one could have a better family than you.

Thanks to my friends – Cleber, Thalita , Popov, Bethany, "Barth," Jeremy Buker and Brett Arp (who was my "wiser half" for so long) – for keeping me grounded and smiling. And especially to my brother, Pedro, who gave me the opportunity to begin again. Thanks, Joe and Joel, for the Virginia memories.

There were so many people involved in the writing of a book like this. My friend and editor, Juli Baldwin, patiently stitched together my thoughts into paragraphs and chapters. This book would not exist without her skill. Tom Bentley and Joel Canfield started me on this journey. They read my original manuscript and encouraged me to be vulnerable enough to write about my darkest hours. Tom Searcy read the first chapters before they were shined up and empowered me with his confidence. So did Barbara Weaver Smith. Their kind words helped me strive for impact.

There were dozens of people who helped take this book from idea to production. Designers, marketing teams, printing experts – the list is long, and I am grateful for all of their efforts. They entertained every wild idea I had (like adding "smell" to the book) and gave me options and ideas. Thank you.

Finally, thanks to you, my readers. This book was years in the making. Every time I wanted to give up, I would read your emails to me about how much your life was changed by one of my articles or blog posts. And that would inspire me to dig deeper. To be more vulnerable. Thank you for the EDGY conversations over the years.

WHO IS THIS
WALDSCHMIDT GUY?

You probably turned to this page because you're thinking, *"Who is this Dan guy, and why should I listen to him? What does he know about success?"*

Fair questions. Now, I'd much rather talk about you than me, but since you asked, I'll answer.

Honestly, I'm just an ordinary guy with an outrageous way of thinking.

It all started more than 30 years ago. I was born five weeks late, and I've been making up for lost time ever since.

I started a lawn-mowing business at age 12 and turned it into a money-making machine (hint: that's the start).

In high school, I ran track and pushed myself until I broke the school's mile record (more conquering).

I also won a national speech contest. I haven't shut up since.

I was 18 when I became the youngest department manager of the Sears in Shelby, NC.

I sold cemetery plots and insurance while studying theology at seminary. (It's good to keep life in perspective.)

Next I got an entry-level sales job with a professional services firm. I changed their sales process, earned millions of dollars for the company and became the CEO at age 25.

And then, I came within a trigger-pull of losing it all. And I learned as much about life and failure as I had about success.

These days, I'm what they call a "business strategist." I head up a company that solves complex problems for organizations all over the world. What I really do is ask the tough questions and talk about the uncomfortable truths no one else is willing to bring up.

I refuse to accept business as usual. And I don't let my clients accept it either. They will tell you that I have some unconventional – but highly effective – ideas about business.

I started writing my blog, *EDGY Conversations*, in 2005. I won't lie – it was gratifying when Dow Jones called it one of the top 7 sales blogs on the web.

And it's pretty fun when the folks at *Business Week, INC Magazine, Business Insider* and the BBC (and a bunch of other magazines, TV and radio shows that you don't care about) want to hear and write about my unconventional ideas.

Remember that speech contest in high school? It set the stage for EDGY keynotes where I challenge people's preconceived notions and totally disrupt the typical business dialogue.

Oh yeah...and sometimes I do some outrageous things.

Like the time I trained for months for an ultimate fighting event. Ultimately the only thing I ended up fighting was a staph infection in the ER. (I'm pretty sure it was a blessing in disguise.)

Now I run ultra-marathons instead. Heck, last year I tried to break the world record for the most miles run in 24 hours. Yeah, I know...insane.

I've also been known to listen to Josh Groban's "You Raise Me Up" 50 times in one day. And I bought Susan Boyle's CD the day it came out. What can I say? I'm a sucker for inspirational music and ugly-duckling success stories. And I always root for the underdog.

If you want to talk with me, lace up your running shoes and hit the roads around Greenville, SC.

I'll be the crazy dude running against traffic.

GET EDGY

CAN'T GET ENOUGH OF DAN?

Follow him on Twitter @DanWaldo. Friend him on Facebook. Connect with him on LinkedIn. Google him. He's everywhere.

WANT TO BE INSPIRED?

Check out EDGYQuotes.com for EDGY ideas worth sharing.

NEED A WEEKLY DOSE OF EDGYNESS?

Get the *EDGY Conversations* blog. Dow Jones calls it one of the top business spots on the web. DanWaldschmidt.com/blog

THINK YOU'RE EDGY?

Find out how EDGY you really are. Answer a few questions, get an EDGY score. Take it again later to see how much EDGY-er you've become. EDGYAudit.com

WONDER WHY YOUR BUSINESS IS BROKEN?

We think we know why...and what you need to do about it. Check out our radical philosophy for business success and industry domination. EDGYManifesto.com

WANT TO STRETCH YOUR TEAM'S THINKING?

Dan will challenge your preconceived notions of what is possible. EDGY keynotes mix his powerful perspective on business growth with raw and gritty inspiration about the deeply personal side of explosive performance. WaldschmidtPartners.com

READY TO START A DIALOGUE WITH DAN?

Dan understands how to ask the tough questions, exposing weaknesses most of us are too afraid to tackle head on, and gets in the trenches with solutions that deliver big results. WaldschmidtPartners.com or dan@danwaldschmidt.com